A Message from the

MW01491918

Congratulations! Right now you are holding one of the key facto *License! Quick Facts for Nursing School®* is our newest study gu ~~~~~~~~ is designed to give you Core Content in a simple, easy-to-understand, "no nonsense" structure that will help you quickly identify your strengths and analyze areas of weakness. With this one book you will immediately begin to comprehend many of the major areas that are essential to learning the art and science of nursing.

YOUR SUCCESS IN NURSING

As you embark on this fulfilling and challenging career path, it's crucial to equip yourself with the knowledge and skills that will make you a competent and confident nurse. That's why I want to emphasize the importance of learning from our reference guide, *Quick Facts for Nursing School®,* and how it can provide you with a strong foundation for your nursing practice.

First and foremost, Quick Facts for Nursing School is designed specifically for nursing students like yourself. It will concisely cover the topics and concepts needed to grasp your nursing education.

One of the key advantages of the Quick Facts for Nursing School® book is its question-and-answer format. This format is a powerful study tool that can significantly enhance your learning experience and save you time. By presenting information in a question-and-answer format, the book engages your active learning process. It prompts you to actively recall information and reinforce your understanding of key concepts. This approach promotes efficient studying and enables you to cut your studying time in half. It covers a wide range of nursing topics, including anatomy and physiology, pharmacology, nursing procedures, medical terminology, and more. The comprehensive nature of this guide ensures that you have a solid foundation of knowledge to build upon as you progress through your nursing classes and enter the professional nursing field.

Another benefit of our Quick Facts for Nursing School book is its portability and convenience. As a nursing student, you'll often find yourself with limited time and in various learning environments. Whether you're studying at home, in the library, or on the go, having a compact and comprehensive resource like *Quick Facts for Nursing School®* allows you to access vital information whenever and wherever you need it.

Wishing you success in your nursing journey!

Regina M. Callion MSN, RN
www.ReMarNurse.com

Scan to Get All Things Social @ ReMarReview

The ReMar Review Quick Facts for Nursing School®

S.M.C. Medical Media

Ordering Information:

Quantity sales- Special discounts are available on quantity purchases by educational institutions, not-for-profits, corporations, associations, and others. For details, contact the publisher at the address above.

Orders by U.S. & International trade bookstores and wholesalers. Please contact ReMar Review:

Email us: Support@ReMarReview.com or visit www.ReMarNurse.com

Medical Disclaimer: The information contained in this book is intended for educational purposes only and is the opinion of the author. It is not intended to be a substitute for professional and medical advice, diagnosis, or treatment. Always seek the advice of your physician or other qualified healthcare provider with any questions you may have regarding a medical condition. Never disregard professional medical advice or delay in seeking it because of something your read. The author does not recommend or endorse any specific tests, physicians, products, procedures, opinions, or other information mentioned in this book.

ISBN: 978-1-961518-01-8

$64.95
ISBN 978-1-961518-01-8
56495>

9 781961 518018

How to use Quick Facts for Nursing School

Quick Facts for Nursing School is designed to be a valuable **reference book** for nursing students to reinforce their understanding of various medical-surgical and pharmacology topics. This section will provide effective strategies on how to study the information presented to you.

Step 1: Set Clear Goals - Before starting your study session, establish clear objectives. Determine which topics you need to focus on before class or what subjects you need to review that were discussed during class.

Step 2: Gather Necessary Materials
- Quick Facts for Nursing School book
- Note-taking supplies (notebook, pens, highlighters, flashcards, or a notebook)
- Laptop or tablet (for additional research if needed)

Step 3: Organize Your Study Space - Choose a quiet and well-lit area free from distractions. Organize your study space to create a comfortable and conducive learning environment.

Step 4: Begin Your Study Session - Start studying the information in the time you have set aside. **Quick Facts for Nursing School is your instant study partner!** This book will ask you the most important questions about the subject. You can begin by just reading the questions and then before looking at the answers, try to recall them. If you do not know the answer on the first pass that is ok. This is why you brought the book, to learn new information.

Sample Study Session with Minute Breakdown

Time	Activity
Pre-Study Session	Go to class or review the class syllabus to know which topics to prepare for
15 minutes	Study a section (example: Amputation)
10 minutes	Review and summarize notes
5 minutes	Study break
10 minutes	Quiz yourself with active recall
5 minutes	Consider how this applies to real life, wrap up your thoughts and move on. Nursing school moves fast and you don't have time to waste.

Step 5: Review and Summarize - As you read through Quick Facts for Nursing School, take notes or highlight key points. Summarize each section in your own words to reinforce your understanding.

Step 6: Quiz Yourself - After reviewing a section or a page, quiz yourself on the material again. Create flashcards or practice questions based on the content you've just studied.

Step 7: Active Recall - Test your memory recall with identifying key points without looking at the book. This technique strengthens long-term retention.

Step 8: Application & Critical Thinking - Apply what you've learned to real scenarios and patient care situations.

Step 9: Take Breaks -Taking short breaks during your study session can help maintain focus and prevent burnout.

Step 10: Reflect and Plan - At the end of your study session, take a few moments to reflect on what you've learned. Consider what you need to review in the next session and set goals for your future study sessions. Remember the goal of this process is not for you to just memorize the information but instead have a basic understanding of the subject matter.

Step 11: Stay Consistent - Consistency is key to effective studying. Schedule regular study sessions using this method to maximize your understanding and retention of the material.

By following this guide and using the Quick Facts for Nursing School book, you can efficiently study medical-surgical topics and enhance your nursing education. Remember to adapt these strategies to your individual learning style and needs. Blessings with your studies!

Do you want to get the most out of this resource?

If you're like me you want to have every bit of information about some before getting started. I've created a quick video resource to give you just that. Scan the code below or go to ReMarNurse.com/STUDY see how you can best integrate this amazing resource with your current nursing school curriculum to build your confidence and master the core nursing content. There's a special way to use this book that will give you the best results and I want to make sure you know exactly what to do, and when to do it!

Table of Contents

ABO Blood Groups

What is the ABO antigen system?	It is the different classes of human blood.
What part of the blood is classified?	The red blood cells are distinguished.
What other blood is compatible with Type A?	Type A +/- or O +/-
What other blood is compatible with Type B?	Type B +/- or O +/-
What other blood is compatible with Type O?	Type O + or O -
What other blood is compatible with Type AB+?	All blood types
What other blood is compatible with Type AB-?	Type AB-, A-, B-, O-

Absorption Factors

These are factors that affect the absorption of medication into the body.

Route of Medication	Affected by
Inhalation	Blood flow to the area, tissue perfusion.
Intramuscular	Blood flow to the muscle, Fat content of the muscle, temperature of the muscle (cold causes vasoconstriction, heat causes vasodilation)
Intravenous	None: Direct entry into the venous system
Mucous membranes (sublingual, buccal)	Blood flow to the area, integrity of the mucous membranes, presence of food, smoking, length of time on the area
Oral (PO)	Blow flow to the GI tract Acidity of the stomach Presence of interacting drugs (ex. Antacids) Length of time in the stomach
Rectal (PR)	Blood flow to the rectum Lesions in the rectum
Subcutaneous	Blood flow to the tissue Fat content of the tissue Temperature of the tissue
Topical	Perfusion or blood flow to the area Integrity of the skin

Acquired Immunodeficiency Syndrome

What is the virus that causes AIDS?	Human Immunodeficiency Virus (HIV)
How is HIV transmitted?	Sexual intercourse direct contact with infected blood or body fluid such as semen and breastmilk. Also during pregnancy and childbirth.
What are the symptoms of HIV?	Fever, weight loss, night sweats, diarrhea, fatigue, muscle aches, swollen lymph glands.
How is the presence of HIV confirmed?	Screening is done FIRST to specifically see if the HIV antibodies are present.
What is the screening test?	ELISA.
What is ELISA?	It is the enzyme-linked immunosorbent assay. A blood test that uses special enzymes that attach to blood.
What confirms the screening test?	HIV differentiation assay Western Blot is no longer used.

How does HIV attack the body?	It attacks the immune system by destroying T – lymphocytes. The virus also rapidly self-replicate.
What is so important about T-lymphocytes?	T cells help the immune system to recognize and fight pathogens.
What is another name for T-lymphocytes?	CD4 cells, Helper T-cells, Thymocyte
Why is the CD4 count important?	The lower the CD4 count, the more damage the virus has done to the body.
What is a normal CD4 count in a client without HIV?	500-1500 in healthy adults.
What is the normal CD4 count in a client with HIV?	Anything at or above 500 means a client is in good health. If the CD4 count is below 200, the HIV has progressed to AIDS.
If a client's CD4 count is below 200, the client is at risk for what?	Opportunistic infections.
What is a nucleic acid test (NATs)?	This is a test for the viral load of HIV in the blood.
List some opportunistic infections.	-Oral pharyngeal candida infection (mouth fungus) -Kaposi's sarcoma (skin cancer) -Pneumocystis pneumonia -Cytomegalovirus (blindness) -Meningitis -Toxoplasmosis, Tuberculosis
What is the goal of HIV medications? replicating inside of the client.	To interfere with the virus
The most important medication to know for NCLEX is _____?	Zidovudine
Which isolation precautions are used with HIV?	Universal precautions. All blood should be suspected of HIV as clients do not have have to tell anyone they have HIV.
How do isolation precautions change with AIDS?	If the client has a low CD4 count and is at risk of an opportunistic infection: The client should have a - Private room - Reverse isolation - RN/PN should wear gloves, gown, goggles, mask when in direct contact with blood or body fluids.
What are the teaching points for parents who have a child with HIV?	- Clean up body fluid/blood with 10:1 water/bleach ratio. - The child should get all immunizations, except lives vaccines such as: MMR, varicella, & oral poliovirus. - Feed child a high-calorie & protein diet. - Use gloves to change diapers.

Acute Renal Failure

What is the definition of acute renal failure (ARF)?

Sudden loss of kidney function to excrete toxins and regulate fluids and electrolytes.

What are some possible causes of ARF?

Infection, obstruction, shock

There are three phases; say what they are?

Oliguric, diuretic, and recovery phase.

During the oliguric phase, what should the nurse expect to see clinically?

This phase lasts 1 to 2 weeks. A low urine output of less than 400 ml per day, hyperkalemia, hypertension, elevated BUN/creatinine levels, and fluid overload. Hyperphosphatemia, metabolic acidosis, & Uremic symptoms

What two electrolytes will be elevated?

Sodium and phosphate.

The diuretic phase is second; what is expected?

The urine output slowly returns, hypokalemia, hyponatremia, hypotension and hypotension.

What does the recovery phase mean?

The kidneys are recovering through a slow process. The GFR increases which allows urine output to increase. The BUN and creatinine return to normal.

Which is the best diet for a client with ARF?

*Healthy carbs, low protein, & low sodium Also limit intake of phosporus and potassium

What are the nursing interventions?

Fluid restrictions, Daily weights Administer diuretics, Monitor electrolytes

Acne

What is acne?

A chronic skin disorder that starts during pregnancy.

Where is acne located?

Lesions on the face, neck, chest, & shoulders.

What are the types of lesions?

Cysts, Closed comedones (whiteheads) Pustule, Papules, Nodules

When does acne get worse?

When there is a hormonal change like menstruation or pregnancy.

What medication can be used for acne?

See chart below.

Medication	Quick Facts
Isotretinoin	Derivative of vitamin A Side effects: Inflammatory bowel disease, depression, severe birth defects Female clients must take birth control during treatment due to possible birth defects.
Spironolactone	Works by blocking the androgen hormones on the oil producing glands
Oral contraceptives Progestin/estrogen	This is an acne therapy with a combination benefit of birth control. Weight gain, breast tenderness, and nausea are common are side effects.
Antibiotics	Moderate to severe acne may require a reduction of bacteria. Tetracycline is the first choice. Macrolides may be used for those who can't take tetracycline for example pregnant clients.
Salicylic acid	It has antibacterial properties. Skin discoloration (redness) and skin irritation may appear.

What are the patient education points?

Instruct on skin cleansing agents.
Instruct not to pick or squeeze lesions.
Do not scrub the face harshly.

Acute Respiratory Distress Syndrome

What is acute respiratory distress syndrome (ARDS)?

Complication caused by lung injury
where fluid fills up in the alveoli.

What is the most common cause?

Sepsis-a widespread infection in the
blood stream.

What are the other causes?

Shock, trauma, drug overdose,
inhalation of toxic substances.

What is the expected arterial blood gas?

Respiratory acidosis

What are the clinical signs?

Tachypnea (earliest sign)
dyspnea, decreased breath
sounds, pulmonary infiltrates.

What are the treatment protocols?

Mechanical ventilation, fluid management,
Treat the underlying cause of disease.

Addison's Disease

What is the cause?

A low production of hormones by
the adrenal gland (glucocorticoids &
mineralocorticoids).

What are some of the major symptoms?

Lethargy, weakness, and weight loss
GI disturbances, skin pigmentation

What color is the skin of a client with
Addison's disease?

Bronzed colored hyperpigmentation
will be noted. The nurse should assess
the palms, in the creases of skin and
over pressure points.

Will this client be overweight?

No as weight loss is common.

Will the serum blood glucose levels be high or low?

Low, along with the sodium levels.
Salt should be increased in the diet.

Will the serum potassium levels be high or low?

High

What is the treatment?

Lifelong glucocorticoid therapy.

Allergies

Clients allergic to latex may also be
allergic to which foods?

Bananas, kiwi, chestnuts.
Avocadoes, plums, strawberry

What standard hospital equipment contains latex?

Blood pressure cuffs, gloves,
stethoscopes, tourniquets, band aids,
and indwelling catheters.

Clients in which careers are most likely to develop
a latex allergy?

Healthcare workers, hairdressers,
and mechanics

What allergy is contraindicated for IV contrast dye?

Iodine/shellfish allergy.

 Study more at ReMarNurse.com | Join live weekly on YouTube @ReMarNurse

Alzheimer's Disease (AD)

Which neurotransmitter is low in AD?

Acetylcholine levels in the cerebral cortex ACH hormone levels are also lower.

What are the signs of AD?

Mild: DENIAL, unable to do demanding jobs, impaired episodic, memory, learning, and counting.

Moderate: IMPAIRED MEMORY apraxia, aphasia, misplaced belongings, deficit in choosing proper attire.

Severe: SEVERELY IMPAIRED MEMORY, incontinence, no verbal or self-care abilities.

If the Mini-Mental State Examination Score is 19 out of 30 which stage is the client likely in?

Stage II (Moderate) Scores
Normal Cognition 25-30
Stage I (Mild) 19-24
Stage 2 (Moderate) 10-18
Stage 3 (Severe) less than 9

Can AD be detected in blood tests?

No, the diagnosis is confirmed by clinical signs and imaging studies.

Is AD reversible?

AD is irreversible due to the permanent damage and amyloid plaques in the brain.

Which medication is given for the symptomatic treatment of cognition in clients with AD?

Cholinesterase inhibitors

Cholinesterase inhibitors are contraindicated in clients who have _____.

Cardiac issues such as bradycardia

What is sundowning?

Behavioral disturbances that commonly peaks in evening, 2/3 of AD clients have this.

Which medication is recommended for agitation and paranoia?

Selective serotonin reuptake inhibitors.

Which medication should be avoided in AD clients who also have depression?

Benzodiazepines because it worsens gait, agitation & can cause physical dependence.

Amputation

What are the major complications of having an amputation performed?

Infections, skin breakdown, phantom limb pain, and joint contractions.

What is the positioning for post-op care?
-AKA (above the knee) amputation

Elevate first 24 hours, then prone. Place the client in the position twice daily to prevent hip flexion.

-BKA (below the knee) amputation

Elevate foot of bed first 24 hours, then prone position twice daily to prevent hip flexion.

What should the nurse encourage?

The expression of feeling about lost limb.

What is phantom limb pain?

Pain felt in an area that has been amputated.

Study more at ReMarNurse.com | Join live weekly on YouTube @ReMarNurse

Amyotrophic Lateral Sclerosis

This condition is also known as?

Lou Gehrig's disease

What happens to the ALS patient?

A progressive neuro- degenerative disease that affects nerve cells in the brain and spinal cord. It affects voluntary control of the arms, legs, & leads to trouble breathing.

Does it affect mental status?

No, it does not.

Is this condition contagious?

It is not contagious.

What are the clinical findings?

Twitching, cramping of the muscles in the hands and feet. Tripping and falling. Dropping things, fatigue, Uncontrollable periods of laughing or crying, slurred or thick speech, troubled breathing, swallowing, and paralysis.

How is ALS diagnosed?

Muscle/nerve biopsy
Blood/urine
Thyroid function tests
Lumbar puncture
MRI

Does it have a cure?

There is no cure. Treatment focuses on minimizing the symptoms.

Anemias

Type of Anemia	Signs	Treatment
Aplastic Anemia	Decreased erythrocytes Bleeding mucous membranes Thrombocytopenia	Antilymphocyte globulin (ALG) Blood transfusions Bone marrow transplantations
Iron Deficiency Anemia	Low hemoglobin & hematocrit Pallor, fatigue, Tissue hypoxia Tachycardia *This is the most common & expected during pregnancy.	Iron supplements Dietary changes-iron rich foods include dark green leafy vegetables, dried fruits, and iron fortified cereals.
Vitamin B 12 (Pernicious Anemia)	Pallor, "beefy red tongue" fatigue, paresthesia	Cyanocobalamin is a manufactured version of vitamin B12. Cyanocobalamin injections are needed to help the body make red blood cells. Dietary changes
Sickle Cell Anemia	See Table of Contents	Can. Will. Must Pass NCLEX!

Aneurysm

True or False? An aneurysm is a dilation formed at a weak point on the wall artery.

True.

What are the symptoms of aneurysms inside the body?

Most aneurysms inside the body do not have symptoms.

What sound would be heard on auscultation?

A blowing bruit is heard.

What are some of the risk factors?

Arteriosclerosis, infection (tertiary stage of syphilis), hypertension, smoking.

What is the treatment for an aneurysm?

Surgery is an option. Strict blood pressure with medications.

What are the signs of a ruptured aneurysm?

Severe pain, N/V, tachycardia, decreased LOC, hypotension.

List important patient teaching points.

Avoid straining, lifting, or exerting, take medications on schedule, report severe back and flank pain.

Anorexia Nervosa

The primary symptom of illness is?	Starvation.
What is the mental perception of the body?	Distorted
At what age does this disease occur?	Adolescent or teenage years
What is the usual personality type?	A perfectionist or overachiever with low esteem.
What is a major cardiac complication of anorexia?	Cardiac arrhythmias
What is a major gynecological complication of anorexia?	Amenorrhea
What is the treatment of anorexia nervosa?	Small, frequent meals with counseling and milieu therapy.

Anxiety Disorders

How is anxiety disorder presented?	Generalized anxiety disorder is characterized by chronic unrealistic and excessive anxiety and worry. *It is an overreaction to something that is real.
Anxiety disorder with recurring thoughts and/or repetitive, ritualistic type behaviors that the individual is unable to keep from doing is defined as _____.	Obsessive Compulsive Disorder
Social anxiety disorder is characterized by:	When interacting or exposed to people: blushing, sweating, trembling, tachycardia.
Which neurotransmitter is believed to be dysfunction in anxiety disorders?	Gamma-aminobutyric acid.
What behavioral therapy teaches the client to create positive messages for use during panic episodes?	Positive reframing
_____ is directed to help the client to take more control over life situations.	Assertiveness training.
_____ is the drug of choice for anxiety disorder however contraindicated in ____ _____.	Benzodiazepines are the drug for anxiety disorder however, contraindicated in clients with narrow angle glaucoma.

Appendicitis

Which age range is the most affected with the condition?	10-30 years old.
What is the most common sign of appendicitis?	Acute right lower abdominal pain
What are other signs and symptoms?	Loss of appetite, nausea, vomiting, low-grade temperature
The localized tenderness is found where?	McBurney's point
What are the tests to determine appendicitis?	Complete history and physical exam with WBC count -the WBC results will be elevated.

What is the treatment for appendicitis?	Immediate surgery to remove appendix, IV antibiotics, semi- fowler's position. A NPO diet to rest the stomach.
What are the general treatments for any acute abdominal pain?	NPO status, no heat on the abdomen assess abdominal distention, IV fluid therapy to prevent hydration.

Arterial Blood Gas

Why would a blood gas be ordered for a patient?	Respiratory distress, management of Mechanical ventilation, shock, trauma, ingestion of poison, DKA
Where are most samples drawn from?	The radial artery in the wrist.
How long should pressure be applied to the site after collecting a sample?	5 minutes
What might be turned off before an ABG?	Oxygen if the doctor orders a room air test.
Which test should be performed before collecting an ABG on a client?	Allen's Test
What is a quick non-invasive substitute?	Pulse oximetry reading will tell a quick measurement of oxygenation status.
What should the sample be placed in immediately?	Ice.

ABG Labs	Normal Value	Meaning
pH	7.35-7.45	Concentration of hydrogen ions (H+) in the blood.
PaO_2	10.7-13.3 kPa	Partial pressure of O2 in arterial blood
$PaCO_2$	35-45 mm Hg	Partial pressure of carbon dioxide in arterial blood.
BE	-2 to +2 mmol/L	Excess or deficit of bicarbonate in blood.
HCO_3-	22- 26 mEq/L	Concentration of bicarbonate in the blood
SaO_2	93-100% *(may vary)*	Percentage of oxygen in hemoglobin.

If the pH is less than 7.35 is it alkalosis or acidosis?	Acidosis
If the pH is more than 7.45 is it alkalosis or acidosis?	Alkalosis

Disorder	pH 7.35-7.45	HCO₃ 22-26	PaCO₂ 35-45
Respiratory Acidosis	↓	↑	↑
Respiratory Alkalosis	↑	↓	↓
Metabolic Acidosis (all arrows going in the same direction)	↓	↓	↓
Metabolic Alkalosis (all arrows going in the same direction)	↑	↑	↑

Disorder	Conditions as a cause	Drugs as a cause
Respiratory Acidosis	COPD, drug overdose, asthma, hypoventilation	Opiates, morphine, sedatives, muscle relaxants
Respiratory Alkalosis	Fever, anxiety, aspirin, poisoning, hyperventilating, anemia	Salicylate, excessive artificial ventilation
Metabolic Acidosis	Severe diarrhea, diabetes mellitus, strenuous exercise, lactic acidosis, renal failure, liver failure	Methanol, ethylene glycol, salicylates
Metabolic Alkalosis	Vomiting, alkaline drugs, continuous gastric content suctioning	Antacids and other bicarbonate containing preparation

Asthma

An obstructive airway disease caused by _____ and _____ of the bronchioles?

Spasms, inflammation

What are the signs of asthma?

Shortness of breath, expiratory wheezes, and possibly a cough.

When will the client experience the cough?

At night

What is the primary treatment goal?

To identify the allergen

Which medications work best for treatment?

Anti-inflammatory, corticosteroids bronchodilators, leukotriene modifiers and metered dose inhalers.

Is albuterol a long term treatment option?

No, it is only going to be effective for a short period of time then it will not reduce reduce symptoms.

Which should a nurse give first—the steroid or Bronchodilators when treating asthma?

Bronchodilator first to open the airway.

When treating a patient long-term with steroids what are they at risk for?

Cushing's syndrome

What are leukotriene modifiers?

They are drugs used to block the chemical leukotriene, which reduces inflammation.

STEPS TO USE A METERED DOSE INHALER

1. Remove the cap.
2. Shake the inhaler well before use.
3. Breathe out and away from the inhaler.
4. Bring the inhaler to the mouth. Place it in mouth between the teeth and close mouth around it.
5. Start to breathe in **slowly**. Press the top of the inhaler once and keep breathing in slowly until one has taken a full breath (three to five seconds).
6. Remove the inhaler from the mouth and hold the breath for about 10 seconds, then breathe out.

*If the client cannot tolerate a bitter taste or is experiencing side effects, they may need a spacer.
*Clients should rinse mouth after each dose to prevent thrush. *Client should wait only one minute between each puff.

Autism Spectrum Disorder

What is autism?

A developmental disorder that impairs the ability to communicate and changes the behavior.

Why is it a "spectrum" disorder?

There is a wide variation in the type and severity of symptoms of each individual.

What are some subtypes?

Asperger disorder, Kanner autism, high functioning, early infantile.

When is the diagnosis usually made?

At ages 2 or 3.

What are some conditions associated with ASD?

See chart below on following page.

Condition	Characteristic
Angelman syndrome	Global developmental delay, hypotonia, wide-based ataxic gait, seizures, progressive spasticity
Tourette syndrome	Tics seen in Tourette syndrome may appear similar to motor stereotypes associated with ASD. Children with Tourette syndrome usually lack social/communication skills impairments seen with ASD; however, social isolation may be a factor due to embarrassment or peer avoidance.
Attention deficit-hyperactivity disorder (ADHD)	Children with ADHD may have impairments in social skills and may have difficulty sustaining conversation due to inattention. Likewise, children with ASD often have problems with hyperactivity, impulsivity, and inattention.
Cornelia de Lange syndrome	Growth delays, intellectual disability, and/or developmental delays and behavioral problems. Children also may have hearing impairment and abnormal speech development.

What is the treatment for autism?

Speech therapy, physical therapy and occupational therapy. Currently there are no medications that can cure the condition.

What are some medication therapies for ASD?

See chart below.

Medication/Therapies	Improvement Noted
Melatonin	Sleep duration
B6/magnesium	Social interaction, communication, repetitive behavior *may cause diarrhea
Music therapy	Improve communication, engagement
Massage	Improve attachment; decrease overarousal
L-Carnosine	Neuroprotective, Improves Receptive/expressive language

What does treatment improve?

Communication and the client's social skills. The goal of treatment is to minimize core deficits and maximize functional independence.

Autonomic Dysreflexia

Autonomic dysreflexia occurs in clients with what type of an injury?

A spinal cord injury (T-6 or above)

What can cause autonomic dysreflexia?

Stimuli such as a full bladder or fecal impaction.

Why is autonomic dysreflexia so serious?

It is life threatening due to clients becoming extremely HYPERTENSIVE.

What is the most common cause of it?

Urinary obstruction

What are the signs of autonomic dysreflexia?

Increase in the BP by 40 mm Hg, headache, bradycardia, blurred vision, & sweating.

What should be done during an episode?

1st place client in high fowler's check for bladder distention. Loosen restrictive clothing.

What is the treatment?

Removal of the stimuli. Client needs to void or have a bowel movement as fecal impaction may be present.

Basic Unit of Measurements

System	Solid Measure	Liquid Measure
Metric	Gram (g) 1 milligram (mg)= 0.001 g 1 microgram (mcg)= 0.000001 g 1 kilogram (kg) = 1,000 g	Liter (L) 1 milliliter (mL) = 0.001 L 1 mL – 1 cubic centimeter = 1 cc
Apothecary	grain (gr) 60 gr= 1 dram (dr) 8 dr = 1 ounce (oz)	minim (min) 60 min = 1 fluidram (fl dr) 8 fl dr = 1 fluid ounce (fl oz)
Household	Pound (lb) 1 lb = 16 ounces (oz) 1 lb= 2.2 kg	Pint (pt) 2 pt = 1 quart (qt) 4 qt = 1 gallon (gal) 16 oz = 1 pt = 2 cups 32 tablespoons (tsbp) =1 pt 3 teaspoons (tsp) = 1 tbsp 60 drops (gtt) = 1 tsp

Bell's Palsy

Bell's palsy affects which cranial nerve?

Cranial nerve #7 or facial nerve

What does the client with Bell's palsy suffer from?

Temporary facial paralysis that affects chewing, eating, and closing of the eyes.

What is the treatment for Bell's palsy?

- Wear an eye patch at night
- Use artificial tears
- Wear glasses to protect eyes
*Steroids to reduce edema & swelling

Benign Prostatic Hyperplasia (BPH)

BPH is cause by _____?

The cause is unknown, but it's an enlargement of the prostate gland.

Because the prostate blocks the urethra opening, what will clients feel and see when they urinate?

Straining to urinate, decreased urine stream, feeling like they have to go all the time, dribbling urine.

Who usually gets BPH?

Men usually over 50

What is the best way to assess for BPH?

Digital rectal exam, physician will feel a pea-sized nodule. A blood test to detect the prostate specific antigen- (PSA). A urine test.

What is the common surgical treatment for BPH?

Transurethral resection of the prostate (TURP)

How is a TURP performed?

A scope goes through the penis and removes parts of the prostate.

After the procedure, what is the client at risk for?
All clients will get a ___ ____ ___ ___ before a TURP.

Bleeding; monitor for hemorrhage.
Three-way (lumen) indwelling catheter.

What are the three lumens for?

Inflating the balloon, inflow of the solution, and outflow of the urine.

What will the doctor order to be done after a TURP?

Continuous Bladder Irrigation (CBI)

What is the goal of a bladder irrigation?	To reduce & prevent blood clots in the post-op client.
Will an incision be made during the irrigation?	No, the irrigation will be done using the indwelling catheter.
What type of fluid is used to irrigate the bladder?	Isotonic sterile saline
What color should the urine be?	Light pink during the procedure that turns to clear.
During CBI what must the client be monitored for?	Bladder distention, fluid overload, *hyponatremia, and blood loss.
If bladder spasms occur, give _____ or _____.	Belladonna/opium suppositories or oxybutynin.
The best position for this client post-op is?	Lying flat because sitting up puts pressure on the bladder.
List client education discharge instructions.	Drink two to three liters of fluids daily. No lifting or straining. If bright red blood clots are present, call the doctor. Do Kegel exercises to strengthen pelvis muscles.

Blindness and Communication with the Visually Impaired

What are the common types of vision loss?	Cortical/Cerebral visual impairment, retinitis pigmentosa, macular degeneration, retinopathy of prematurity.
Which act mandates health facilities provide access to communication for clients with disabilities?	American Disabilities Act. It also guides nurses to prevent discrimination.
True or False: It is the nurse who decides the preferred method of communication.	False. The nurse must ask the client's preferred method of communication.
How do you communicate to clients with vision loss only?	Clear and direct verbal response. Make sure to describe the environment or the procedure.
What is the deaf-blind communication method where the person places their hands on the speaker's jaw, bottom lip, or neck to feel the vibrations?	Tactile lip reading or tadoma.
What tactile writing system used by clients with vision loss?	Braille. It has several types such as braille on paper, braille display and finger braille.
What tactile method which the nurse uses his/her finger to write letters in the palm of the client?	Print on palm. Letters are written down on the client's palm for him/ her to read.
True or False: Dactylology is not indicated as a communication for a client with vision loss.	False. Fingerspelling or dactylology uses hands to represent the letters of writing system, and number systems. Words are spelled out where the client places a hand over the signer.

Blood Administration

What must be received before a blood transfusion is started?	A signed written consent
Which blood type is considered universal and can be used for all other donors?	Type O Negative
What blood type is considered the universal recipient and can receive all blood types?	Type AB Positive
What is the most common infection spread through blood transfusions?	Hepatitis B
In order to determine donor compatibility, what test must be done?	Type and crossmatch
What must be done to determine a client's baseline before starting the transfusion?	Take the vital signs
What size IV gauge must the client have?	18G with a filter needle
How many nurses confirm the unit of blood?	2
How long after blood is removed from the blood bank's refrigerator should it be started?	30 minutes.
How long must a nurse stay with the client after the transfusion is started?	15 minutes
How many mLs are in one unit of packed red blood cells?	About 250 mL
What are the signs of an adverse reaction?	Restlessness, nausea, hives, SOB, fever, chills, back pain.
Why is blood administered at a slow rate?	Because running blood fast can cause fluid overload in Clients.
Which drug is also used to treat anemia because it increases red blood cell production?	Epoetin alfa
Clients taking Epoetin alfa should be monitored for what?	Hypertension and seizures

Blood Pressure

What is a blood pressure?	The force of blood flowing through the arteries.
What is the recommended blood pressure?	120/80 for adults 90/60 for children 70/40 for infants
What are the top and bottom values?	Systolic and diastolic pressure
Define the terms: systolic and diastolic pressure.	Systolic: Pressure while heart beats. Diastolic: Pressure while heart is at rest.
Which value determines if a person has HTN?	Diastolic - If the pressure of the heart is elevated at rest, then hypertension is present.

What are the risk factors for hypertension?

African Americans, obesity, anxiety, diabetes mellitus type 2, and a smoking history

What are the physical signs of hypertension?

Blurry vision, headache, chest pain; but remember that HTN is called a silent KILLER as most people don't have symptoms.

How can the size of the blood pressure cuff affect the blood pressure reading?

If it's too small, the BP will be higher than it really is. If the cuff is too big, the BP will be lower than it actually is.

What are some other factors that alter blood pressure?

Position of the client, caffeine intake, anxiety, and activity.

What is pulse pressure?

The difference between systolic and diastolic numbers.

What is the mean arterial pressure?

Diastolic pressure (+) 1/3 of pulse pressure; this value should be greater than 60.

Before a blood pressure medication is given, always check _____ _____ and _____ _____?

Blood pressure and pulse rate

Hold the medication if systolic BP is less than _____ or heart rate is less than _____.

100, 60

Which classes of medications are used for HTN?

Diuretics, beta blockers, calcium channel blockers, and vasodilators.

Medications that end in "pril" are _____ _____?

Ace inhibitors, captopril, enalapril

Ace inhibitors correct heart failure by _____ after load?

Decreasing - they also promote vasodilation by inhibiting the production of angiotensin.

_____ is an adverse reaction seen with the use of ACE inhibitors.
Signs of angioedema are?
Clients may also have a persistent, nagging _____.

Angioedema

Swelling of the lips and mouth
Cough

Which is more dangerous in angioedema: a cough or swelling of the lips and mouth?

Swelling of the lips and mouth may indicate laryngeal angioedema. A compromised airway is the priority.

Medications that end in "olol" are ___ ___?

Beta blockers, metoprolol, carvedilol

Clients who take anti-hypertensive medications and sit in a chair or at a bedside should be taught what method to avoid falling?

Sit for 30 minutes after taking medication to adjust to a lower circulating blood pressure.

Which herbal medication is used to lower BP?

Garlic.

Clients taking anti-hypertensives should avoid hot showers, baths, and weather. True or false?

True. These things can cause dizziness.

What is the best diet for a hypertensive client?

Low-sodium, low-fat DASH diet.

 Study more at ReMarNurse.com | Join live weekly on YouTube @ReMarNurse

Body Mass Index (BMI)

Body Mass Index Parameter	Normal Values
Underweight	Less than 18.5 kg/m2
Normal	18.5-24.9 kg/m2 (Caucasian)
Overweight	25.0-29.9 kg/m2
Obesity class 1	30.0-34.9 kg/m2
Obesity class 2	35.0-39.9 kg/m2
Obesity class 3 (extreme, morbid)	Over 40 kg/m2

What are the implications of a high BMI?

A high BMI is associated with various health problems including: hypertension, heart disease, diabetes mellitus, sleep apnea, fatty liver disease, depression, social stigma.

What are the implications of a low BMI?

A low BMI can indicate malnutrition and other conditions such as a weakened immune system, impaired wound healing, decreased muscle mass, increased risk of osteoporosis and fractures, menstrual irregularities in females.

What are the limitations of a BMI

as a health assessment tool?

The limitations include the fact that it does not differentiate between muscle mass and fat mass. It is not applicable to children, older adults etc. It does not account for differences in body composition based on ethnicity or gender.

Bronchiolitis

What is the peak age for this condition?

Young infants.

What are the clinical symptoms?

Viral infections, thick secretions, paroxysmal coughing, shallow rapid respirations, nasal flaring.

What is the most common cause?

Respiratory syncytial virus

Is there a vaccine available?

No there is not. The medication for treatment is palivizumab.

What is the management?

Contact isolation, hydration, mist tent with oxygenation, clear airway of secretions.

Bronchitis

What is bronchitis?

Bronchitis happens when the airways of the lungs swell and produce mucus.

What organs are commonly affected?

The trachea and bronchi are inflamed.

What is the most common type of bronchitis?

Acute bronchitis or chest cold is the most common type.

What are the symptoms of bronchitis?

Hyperthermia, fatigue, dry hacking cough that worsens at night. There can also be watery eyes, sore throat, headache. Mucus will also be produced.

What causes bronchitis?	A bacteria or virus that causes an upper respiratory infection.
What is the treatment for bronchitis?	Rest, hydration for self-care, antibiotics for bacterial infections, guaifenesin for cough and to loosen mucus. Albuterol may also be prescribed.

Breast Cancer

What are the common types of breast cancer?	Invasive or non-invasive. Invasive means cancerous, malignant, or spreads to other organs. Non-invasive is still in the original position.
What is the most common form of breast cancer?	Invasive ductal carcinoma
What are the risk factors?	Age, gender, family history, oral contraceptive use, obesity, breast density, smoking.
What are the signs of breast cancer?	A lump in the breast or under the arm. A change in the size of the breast. Skin irritation, breast pain, nipple tenderness, and nipple discharge other than milk.
Where is breast cancer most likely to occur?	The upper outer quadrant where most breast tissue is located.
What are the diagnostic evaluations?	Mammogram, ultrasound, biopsy.
What biomarker determines the rate of tumor growth?	Ki-67 is a nuclear protein. That shows the growth rate.
What are the treatment options?	Surgery, radiation, chemotherapy, hormone therapy.
What is considered local therapy?	Surgery & radiation
What stage of breast cancer is radiation therapy no longer recommended?	Stage IV
What is a lumpectomy?	Removal of the tumor or malignant tissue.
What is a mastectomy?	Removal of the entire breast. Bilateral mastectomy is when both breasts are removed.
What are the post-surgical implications?	If axillary lymph nodes are removed swelling of the arm & chest may occur (lymphedema). Elevate the extremity to decrease swelling, an icepack may be used. Avoid measuring blood pressure, venipuncture, or vascular access on the affected arm to reduce the risk of lymphedema. Administer pain medication.
What are the nursing interventions?	Monitor for adverse effects. Radiation: fatigue, sore throat, dry cough, nausea and vomiting Chemotherapy: bone marrow suppression, nausea, vomiting, alopecia, weight loss, stomatitis, anxiety, and depression. Provide emotional support. Encourage the yearly mammograms starting at age 40.

Breast Feeding

Breast feeding moms will often feel what while feeding the baby?	Abdominal cramps.
Abdominal cramps are due to the release of?	Prolactin and oxytocin
What is the best way to burp a baby?	While he/she is sitting up
What is the infection of the breast tissue called?	Mastitis
What is the treatment for mastitis?	Antibiotics such as penicillin
What are the benefits of breastfeeding?	Passive immunity, quicker weight loss in mother after birth, increase in bonding, economically a no cost food.

Buerger's Disease (Thromboangiitis Obliterans)

This disease is the obstruction and inflammation of blood vessels mainly where?	In the hands and feet.
What are the clinical symptoms?	Pale, blue, hands and feet; they may tingle or be painful. They will be cold.
Who is most at risk for this disease?	Males who smoke or chew tobacco.
What are the treatment goals?	There is no cure, only symptom control; teach clients to stop smoking, dress appropriately for the weather, and try to reduce life stressors.

Bulimia Nervosa

What is the eating cycle involved?	Eating binges followed by purging of all the foods consumed.
Will you be able to see physical changes or weight loss?	The client usually remains at a normal weight.
Besides purging, what other methods are used to lose weight?	Vomiting, enemas, drugs diuretics, diets, and laxatives.
What are the medical complications associated with bulimia nervosa?	Tooth decay, electrolyte imbalances, ulcers, cardiac arrhythmias.
Safety is a concern in clients with bulimia nervosa because of ____ ____.	Suicidal thoughts
List the treatment goals.	Encouraging talking, safety and assessing suicidal potential, establishing a diet plan, supervision during mealtime, and antidepressants may be prescribed.

Do you remember how HIV attacks the body?

You will never change your life until you change something you do daily.
Your daily routine is the bases of your success! ☺

Burns

What are the two age groups most at risk for suffering a burn injury?	Children and the elderly.
What are the four types of burns?	Chemical, electrical, thermal and radiation.
If the face/neck has been burned, what is the nursing priority?	Assess airway obstruction.

*Classification of Burns

1st degree (Superficial partial thickness)	Skin pink/red, painful (e.g., sunburn).
2nd degree (Deep partial thickness)	Skin red/white, blisters, and swelling is noted.
3rd degree (Full thickness)	Skin black/brown, edema, all layers of skin burned, grafting may be needed.
What is the formula used to determine fluid replacement for the first 24 hours?	The parkland formula.
What is the Parkland formula?	4ml of lactated ringer (LR) x weight (kg) x % of body that is burned.
How much of this fluid do you give in the first eight hours?	½ of total volume.
How much fluid do you give for the second eight hours?	¼ of total volume.
How much fluid do you give for the third eight hours?	¼ of total volume.
Should the client burst a blister?	No
Which is the best route for pain medications?	IV
Which diet is appropriate for clients with burns?	High calorie, high protein
What is a common electrolyte problem in clients with burns?	Hypokalemia or hyperkalemia; both can be seen in clients with burned skin.
Due to prolonged stress, clients are at risk For which type of ulcers?	Curling's ulcers.
What medication should be given before dressing changes?	Pain medication

Cancer

True or False? Cancer is an abnormal growth of cells.	True – the growth of cells is uncontrolled.
When the cancer cell travels from the original location to a new place, what is it called?	Metastasis
What acronym is used to describe the warning signs of cancer?	C.A.U.T.I.O.N.
What do the letters stand for?	Change in bowel or bladder Any sore that does not heal Unusual bleeding/discharge Thickening in breast Indigestion Obvious change in a wart Nagging cough or hoarseness
What are the two ways to describe a tumor?	By grading or staging.

What is the difference between the two?

Grading describes a tumor by the cells. Staging describes the progression of a tumor by the clinical symptoms.

What are the three types of radiation treatment?

External unsealed; internal sealed; and internal.

What precautions must be taken for a client receiving radiation treatment?

Private room and a bathroom, limit visitors, rotate nursing staff who provide care, place a sign at door and bedside.

What is the most dangerous type of radiation?

Sealed internal radiation because a solid radioactive implant is placed inside of the tumor.

What additional precautions must be taken for clients receiving sealed internal radiation?

All body fluids are radioactive; use hazardous clean up gloves and gown.

If a client's sealed internal implant falls out. (e.g., cervical implant), what should you do?

Pick it up with long-handle forceps and put it in a lead container.

Chemotherapy works by destroying the cell _____.

Wall

What are the side effects of chemotherapy?

Nausea, anorexia, alopecia sterility, oral thrush, neuropathy, fatigue.

Why is metoclopramide given?

To reduce nausea.

Is alopecia from chemotherapy permanent?

No, it is temporary.

Is sterility from chemotherapy permanent?

Yes

Clients with cancer will also need ____ _____.

Neutropenic precautions

What are neutropenic precautions?

Strict hand washing.
No visitors who are sick.
No children allowed.
No raw food, no live plants.
No free-standing water in the room.

What is filgrastim?

A drug used to treat neutropenia; the nurse should monitor WBCs after administration.

When is the best time to do a breast self-exam?

Once a month however these are no longer recommended due to the harm of false positive results.

When is the best time to do a self-testicular exam?

The same day each month.

Hey, I just wanted to stop in and say got this!

Stay focused and remember your WHY!

You Can. You Will. You Must
Pass Nursing School!

Professor Regina M. Callion MSN, RN

Need more help? Take the Next Gen NCLEX
30-Day Challenge inside the ReMar V2!
ReMarNurse.com/30days

Cardiopulmonary Resuscitation (CPR)

CPR	Infant (up to 1 year)	Child (1 year to signs of puberty)	Older Child & Adult (puberty and older)
Verify Scene Safety	Do not enter an unsafe environment. Call 9-1-1		
Check the victim's responsiveness	If the victim is unresponsive, shout for help. Call 9-1-1 with a mobile device, if outside the hospital. Send someone to find an AED.		
Activate 9-1-1	If the nurse is alone and does not have access to a mobile device leave the victim to call 9-1-1 or activate EMS first, then look for an AED. Return to perform CPR.		
Determine if victim is breathing & has a pulse	Simultaneously check for breathing and pulse for no more than 10 seconds. Note: Agonal breaths are not considered signs of breathing. For children and infants, a pulse rate of less than 60 beats/minute is treated as no pulse.		
	Check brachial artery on the inside of the victim's upper arm near the armpit	Check the carotid artery on the victim's the neck. Use the side closest to you.	
Rescue breathing If victim has a DEFINITE detectable pulse but is not breathing.	1 breath every 3-5 seconds. Check pulse again every 2 minutes. If pulse is less than 60 beats per minute, or perfusion remains poor add chest compressions.	1 breath every 5-6 seconds. Check pulse every 2 minutes. *For suspected opioid overdose, administer naloxone, if available.	
If the victim has no detectable pulse. BEGIN CPR	1 rescuer: 30 compressions: 2 breaths 2+ rescuers: 15 compressions: 2 breaths Use AED as soon as it arrives	1 rescuer: 30 compressions: 2 breaths 2+ rescuers: 15 compressions: 2 breaths Use AED as soon as it arrives	
Compression rate	100-120 compression per minute		
Hand placement	1 rescuer: 2 fingers 2+ rescuers: 2 thumbs on the center of the chest just below the nipple line.	2 hands on the lower half of the breastbone	
Compression depth	1/3 the depth of the chest about 1.5 inches	2 to 2.4 inches	
Chest recoil	Look for full chest recoil after each compression		

Cardiovascular System

What is another name for the cardiovascular system?

Circulatory system

What is lymph fluid?

A colorless fluid that contains white blood cells.

What is the function of the lymphatic system?

Transport lymph fluid throughout the body using lymph nodes.

Is the lymphatic system open or closed?

Open

What lymphatic organ filters the blood?

Spleen

Is the circulatory system open or closed?

Closed

What are the two closed double loop systems that transport blood?

Systemic loop system and pulmonary loop system

Which of the two closed systems transports deoxygenated blood from the right ventricle and returns oxygenated blood to the left atrium?

Pulmonary loop system

Which of the two closed systems transports oxygenated blood from the left ventricle and returns oxygenated blood to the right atrium?

Systemic loop system

What is the pale-yellow liquid portion of blood that carries red blood cells, white blood cells, and platelets?

Plasma

What is a localized weakening of an artery's wall called?

Aneurysm

What is the event in which there is a blockage of blood flow to the heart muscle?	Heart attack or Myocardial infarction
What are some signs of a heart attack?	Chest pain, jaw pain, squeezing sensation in the chest, shortness of breath nausea, dizziness.
During a myocardial infarction what should placed on the patient?	Oxygen
What is a stroke?	Disease that affects the arteries in the brain.
How are the arteries affected in a stroke?	They are blocked or leaking blood.
What are the signs of a stroke?	Weakness or numbness on one side of the body. Loss of vision, or inability to speak or swallow. Difficulty moving.
What is hypertension?	High blood pressure because the force against arterial wall is high.
What are some causes of hypertension?	Obesity, smoking, old age, genetics stress, too much sodium in diet.
What is the buildup of plaque in the arteries called?	Atherosclerosis
What is the cause of atherosclerosis?	High blood pressure, Smoking, high cholesterol.
When the heart is beating too fast it is called ___?	Tachycardia
When the heart is beating too slow it is called ___?	Bradycardia
When the heart has an irregular rhythm, it is called __?	Arrhythmia
What is the sequence of structures involved in the direction of blood flow?	1. Superior and inferior vena cava 2. Right atrium 3. Tricuspid valve 4. Right ventricle 5. Pulmonic valve 6. Pulmonary artery (*Blood receives oxygen*) 7. Pulmonary vein 8. Left atrium 9. Bicuspid valve 10. Left ventricle 11. Aortic valve 12. Aorta

Cataracts

What are the signs of cataracts?	Milky or white lens painless blurry vision.
How are cataracts treated?	No treatment required until the vision is severely impaired.
During surgery, what is done?	The cataracts are removed and a new lens may be implanted.
After surgery, will the vision be corrected?	Only if a new lens is placed. If no lens is placed, the client will still need glasses or contacts.

After surgery, what is the main concern?

To check for hemorrhage of the eye.
The nurse should place the client in
semi-fowler's position.

What should clients avoid after surgery?

Coughing, sneezing, bending over at the
waist, straining, rubbing eye, or crying.
Also, no lifting weight greater than five pounds.

How should the client sleep after surgery?

They should sleep on the unaffected side.
If surgery was done on both eyes, clients
should sleep on back. The client should use
an eye shield at night to protect the eye.

Celiac Disease

Foods containing _____ must not be eaten

Gluten (This is protein).

In Celiac's disease, malabsorption of _____ occurs.

Fats

What foods contain gluten?

B.R.O.W. (barley, rye, oats, and wheat).

The client's abdomen is often _____.

Distended.

What does the client's stool look like?

Smelly, pale, bulky; expect lots of
gas with some diarrhea.

The best food substitutes are _____
and _____.

Corn, rice.

Can a client on a gluten free diet have
cookies, spaghetti, or waffles?

No, all these products grains/gluten
in them.

What is another name for celiac disease?

Celiac sprue.

Cerebral Palsy

True or False: Cerebral palsy (CP) happens as a
result of brain injury to the fully developed brain?

False, CP is a nonprogressive
injury to the immature brain.

What are the signs in an infant?

Poor head control , > 3 months stiff or rigid
arms/legs, uses one side of the body or
only arms to crawl, tongue thrusting.

When is the earliest age CP is diagnosed?

Diagnosis of CP can be as early as
12 to 18 months.

How is CP diagnosed?

MRI, physical, electroencephalogram
(EEG) vision tests, speech delay test

The most common form of CP is injury
to the upper motor neurons. This is called
_____ _____ _____.

Spastic cerebral palsy

What is the motor impairment of both legs called?

Diplegia

What is tetraplegia?

All four extremities involved

What is hemiplegia?

Motor dysfunction of one side of the body.

What are the slow wormlike movements of the
neck facial muscles and tongue called?

Athetosis

Is the condition reversible?

No

| What medications can be prescribed? | Analgesics to reduce pain. Botulinum toxin type A to reduce spasticity in muscles. Dantrolene sodium to improve muscle coordination. |

| What are the nursing interventions? | Encourage physical therapy occupational therapy with speech therapy. |

Cerebrovascular Accident (CVA)

| Define the term CVA. | Reduction of cerebral blood flow and oxygen which causes brain cell damage. |

| What is another name for a CVA? | A stroke. |

| What are the risk factors? | Hypertension, hyperlipidemia atrial fibrillation, diabetes mellitus, smoking. |

| What increases a woman's risk of having a stroke? | Taking contraceptive pills, hormone replacement therapy and pregnancy. |

The three most common causes of CVA are?

Ischemia- a clot, a fatty plaque deposit that blocks blood flow.

Hemorrhage- a weakened blood vessel that ruptures and bleeds into surrounding brain tissue.

Transient Ischemic attack- a mini stroke caused by clots or blockages that are temporary. A brief interruption of blood supply to the brain.

What are the signs of a CVA?

F-ace drooping.
Ask the client to smile.
Is it uneven?
A-rm weakness
Ask the person to raise both arms.
Does it drift downward?
S-peech difficulty (Is speech slurred?)
T-ime (Call 911 when symptoms are present).

What is the difference between CVA and a transient ischemic attack (TIA)?

TIA is a temporary period of neurological deficit. It has similar signs as a CVA, but the symptoms will all resolve and disappear.

| What is agnosia? | Inability to use an object correctly. |

Expressive aphasia occurs when _____.

The client cannot communicate properly. The aphasia can be expressive or receptive.

| If the left hemisphere of the brain is affected, you will see weakness on the____ side. | Right |

| If the right hemisphere is affected, you will see weakness on the____ side. | Left |

| Remember to place the client's belongings on the _____ side. | Unaffected |

The tests used to determine a CVA are?	CT, EEG, & cerebral arteriography
Clients with hemorrhagic stroke are at an increased risk for which complication?	Seizures due to possible bleeding in the cerebral cortex.
What are the nursing assessments?	Monitor vital signs, neuro checks, watch for seizures, monitor for an increase in cranial pressure, check for the ability to swallow (risk for aspiration).
What complication of the eyes can a client with a CVA have?	Corneal abrasions- as the lacrimal glands will not produce lubrication.
What is the activity level for this client?	Strict bed rest.
How should the room environment be?	Quiet, peaceful, with objects within reach on unaffected side
How do you position the CVA client?	Turn every two hours on the unaffected side, then 20 minutes on the affected side, make sure to elevate affected extremities.
Why would a thrombolytic be given?	To dissolve a clot.
Do not give thrombolytics if the cause of the stroke is _____? What other medications may be prescribed to treat a CVA?	Hemorrhage – this will cause more bleeding in the client. Anti-hypertensives, anti-coagulants (not for a hemorrhagic stroke) and anti-convulsant medications.
Do anti-coagulants like coumadin and aspirin dissolve blood clots?	No, they only thin the blood; they do not dissolve clots in the blood.
What is stroke rehabilitation?	Speech therapy Occupational therapy Physical therapy

Cholelithiasis

What is cholelithiasis?	Gallstones are solid masses formed from bile.
What are the causes?	Increased age, female gender, genetics
What are the usual symptoms?	Biliary colic, cholecystitis, jaundice.
How are gallstones diagnosed?	Through blood tests, ultrasound, CT scans, MRI.
What treatment is available?	Surgery, endoscopic retrograde-cholangio-pancreatography (ERCP), gallbladder removal.

Study more at ReMarNurse.com | Join live weekly on YouTube @ReMarNurse

Chronic Obstructive Pulmonary Disease (COPD)

What are the three disorders that make up COPD?

Asthma, bronchitis, and emphysema.

What are the clinical signs of COPD?

Shortness of breath (SOB), activity, wheezing, a productive cough and cyanosis.

What would the arterial blood gas show?

Hypoxemia

What does the chest of a client with COPD look like?

Barrel chest

What would the fingers of a COPD client look like? Due to SOB with activity clients may experience _____ _____ because of difficulty eating.

Clubbed fingers
Weight loss

Why must you assess the amount of O2 your COPD client receives?

The client keep high levels of carbon dioxide in their blood stream which controls the rate of their breathing.

A client with COPD should not receive O2 by NC greater than _____.

2 LPM

To control SOB, the ___ ___ ___ technique should be taught.

Pursed lip breathing

Chronic Renal Failure

Chronic renal failure is progressive and irreversible. True or False?

True.

What are possible causes of CRF?

Hypertension, frequent infections, diabetes mellitus type 2 and renal obstruction.

What is the normal glomerular filtration rate?

90-120 mL/min

What clinical signs would clients show?

Decreased urine output, hypertension, decreased urine specific gravity, and fluid overload.

What is uremic frost?

Urea crystals that come through the skin with perspiration.

Where would you see this frost?

Face, underarms, groin; teach the client to wash their skin with plain water.

What hormones do the kidneys secrete?

Renin, erythropoietin, calcitriol

What are the nursing interventions for chronic renal failure?

Modification of diet, diuretics anti-hypertensives, monitor BUN & creatinine, and taking a daily weight. The daily weight should be taken at the same time each day.

Clients may need _____ to assist With waste removal in the blood.

Dialysis.

What is the best diet for CRF clients?

Moderate carbohydrate, low protein; the goal of this diet is to provide energy while decreasing protein metabolism.

What complications should the nurse monitor for?

Anemia and renal osteodystrophy

Cirrhosis

What are the 3 common causes of liver cirrhosis?

Viral hepatitis, alcohol consumption, and non-alcohol associated fatty liver disease.

What are the signs of liver cirrhosis?

Jaundice, spider angioma, itchy skin, tiredness, loss of appetite

What is the goal of treatment for liver cirrhosis?

Managing the symptoms and preventing complications

In clients with ascites what type of diet is indicated?

Sodium-restricted

_____ is elevated in clients with hepatic encephalopathy.

Ammonia

Which medications allows for the passage of ammonia from the intestines?

Lactulose; it stimulates the passage of ammonia.

Civil Laws

What is the difference between civil law and criminal law?

Civil law is concerned with the rights obligations, and legal relationships that exist between private citizens. While criminal law is concerned with the punishment of individuals who commit crimes such as felonies, misdemeanors, and infractions. In contrast to criminal law, which requires a jury to find a person guilty beyond a reasonable doubt, civil law merely needs a certainty of guilt of higher than 50 percent. Civil law can affect any nurse depending on activity in regular practice.

True or False: A contract is under civil law.

True. Civil law includes contract law. Contracts are binding written, verbal, or implied agreements.

Is tort law the same as civil law?

Tort law is also included in civil law. A tort is an act of commission or omission that gives rise to injury or harm to another and amounts to a civil wrong for which courts impose liability.

What are the categories of tort in the nursing practice?

Two categories of torts that affect nursing practice are intentional and unintentional torts. Intentional torts are acts that the defendant knew would cause harm. When the defendant's actions or inactions were unreasonably unsafe or result from acts of commission or omission.

True or False: Name-calling is a form of assault.

True. Name-calling is verbal assault. Remember, assault is defined as intentionally putting another person in reasonable apprehension of an imminent harmful or offensive contact.

In order to avoid being charged with assault and and battery while performing the procedures, the nurse must ensure that there is _____ _____.

Informed consent.

What are the types of restraints a nurse can apply?

There are 3 types of restraints used in nursing: physical, chemical and verbal.

To avoid false imprisonment while applying, restraints the nurse should _____.

Read and adhere to the agency's protocol in applying restraints.

A client's health information is safeguarded by the standards of _____.

Health Insurance Portability and Accountability Act. (HIPAA).

Damaging one's reputation by making negative, malicious and false remarks is called _____.

Defamation.

What is the difference between slander and libel?

Slander is a verbal defamation while libel is written.

What is the difference between negligence and malpractice?

Negligence is the failure to exercise the ordinary care reasonable person would use in similar circumstances. Malpractice is a specific term used for licensed professional not delivering a set of professional standard procedures.

What are the 4 elements of malpractice?

Duty – the act was done within the line of duty.
Breach – the standard of care was not met and caused harm.
Cause – injury was due to breach of duty.
Harm – injury resulted in damages.

Conjunctivitis

What causes conjunctivitis?

Typically, infections from a bacteria, fungi, or a virus. Allergens, chemicals, and pollution also could be causes.

What bacteria can cause this?

Staphylococcus aureus, streptococcus pneumoniae, haemophilus influenzae, moraxella catarrhalis, or less commonly, chlamydia trachomatis and Neisseria gonorrhoeae.

Are conjunctivitis and stye the same?

No, a stye is a red, painful bump that forms on the edge of the eyelashes on or within the eyelid. Conjunctivitis does not form bumps in the eyelid or around the eye.

Is this contagious?

Yes, conjunctivitis caused by infections are contagious. Conjunctivitis caused by allergies are not.

What is the incubation period?

24 to 72 hours.

What is the difference between bacterial & viral conjunctivitis?

Bacterial can cause yellow or green sticky discharge from the eyes. Viral causes will produce a clear discharge.

How is conjunctivitis spread?

1. When in close contact with someone with conjunctivitis infected hands, and then touching the eyes).
2. Touching the eyes after coming into contact with a surface contaminated with bacteria or viruses.
3. Using or sharing contaminated cosmetics.
4. Through sexual contact. Contacting infected sperm or vaginal fluid and subsequently touching the eyes.

Does conjunctivitis require treatment?

Antibiotics (eye drops, ointments, or pills) are prescribed if the cause is a bacteria. If the cause is a virus then an anti-viral will be given. Anti-histamine is prescribed for allergic conjunctivitis.

Can conjunctivitis be prevented?

Yes, practicing good hygiene is a way to control conjunctivitis.

Corticosteroids

Most corticosteroids end in _____.

ONE

What are the primary functions of corticosteroids?

To decrease inflammation and hormone replacement

What should you teach clients about stopping? corticosteroid therapy?

To gradually decrease use; don't abruptly stop.

What must be monitored while a client is is taking a steroid?

Potassium levels which will decrease. Glucose levels which will increase. Sodium levels will increase as well as overall fluid retention. This may cause an increase in blood pressure.

Corticosteroids may cause symptoms of _____.

Cushing's syndrome.

Corticosteroids will also delay _____ healing.

Wound

If the client is NPO before surgery should the nurse still give the steroid?

Yes, request the doctor to change the route because surgery can cause additional stress on the body and steroids will help in the recovery process.

Corticosteroids

Short-acting drugs		
Medication	Administration	Duration
Hydrocortisone	Oral, parenteral, topical	8-12 hours
Cortisone	Oral parenteral, topical	8-12 hours

Intermediate-acting drugs		
Medication	Administration	Duration
Methyl-prednisolone	Oral, parenteral, topical	12-36 hours
Prednisolone*	Eye drops, Oral parenteral, topical	12-36 hours
Prednisolone*	Oral prep only	12-36 hours

Long-acting drugs		
Medication	Administration	Duration
Betamethasone	Oral, parenteral	24-72 hours
Dexamethasone	Eye drops, parenteral	24-72 hours

Covid-19

Is the Covid-19 a viral or bacterial condition?

It is a viral condition.

What is the virus called?

Severe acute respiratory syndrome coronavirus 2 (SARS-CoV-2).

How soon do symptoms appear?

Symptoms appear 2-14 days after exposure to the virus

| Which isolation precaution is required? | The mode of transmission is human to human via respiratory droplets. So droplet precaution is required. |

What are the signs of a COVID-19 infection?

Nasal congestion, sneezing, respiratory distress, cough, headache, diarrhea, smell, or taste changes may occur. The spectrum of symptoms range from asymptomatic to life-threatening respiratory failure.

How is COVID-19 diagnosed?

There are 2 types of viral tests used to make the diagnosis of COVID-19.

What are the tests?

1. Nucleic acid amplification Test (NAATs).
2. Antigen tests.

What is the treatment for COVID-19?

Nirmatrelvir-ritonavir is a combination drug that should be administered within five days of symptom onset.

Cranial Nerves

What nerve	What it controls
I Olfactory	Sense of smell
II Optic	Vision
III Oculomotor IV Trochlear VI Abducens	Eye movement
V Trigeminal	Sensations of the face
VII Facial	Expressions of the face
VIII Acoustic	Hearing and balance
IX Glossopharyngeal	Gag and swallow
X Vagus	Gag and parasympathetic muscles
XI Spinal Accessory	Back and neck muscles
XII Hypoglossal	Tongue

The client is unable to shrug his shoulders; which nerve is dysfunctional?

CN X1 Accessory

A client is unable to smell his morning coffee; which nerve is dysfunctional?

CN 1 Olfactory

A client is unable to distinguish between salty and sweet tastes; which nerve is dysfunctional?

CN VII Facial

Which is responsible for the control of the heart rate and digestive system?

CN X Vagus

Crohn's Disease

Crohn's disease is an _____ of the bowels.

Inflammation.

Can Crohn's disease be cured with surgery?

No, symptoms frequently will reoccur.

Crohn's disease affects the digestive tract from the mouth to anus. True of False?

True

What are the symptoms of Crohn's disease?

Abdominal pain, diarrhea, weight loss.

Excessive diarrhea will cause which electrolyte imbalance?

Hypokalemia.

What foods should be avoided and why?	Dairy products and high-fiber meals, which may worsen diarrhea.
Crohn's disease can lead to which kind of cancer?	Colon.
What are the treatment goals?	Drugs and nutrition to reduce inflammation.

Croup

What is croup?	An infection in the upper respiratory tract with inflammation of the larynx trachea, and bronchi.
What is another name for croup?	Laryngotracheobronchitis.
What are common causes?	Respiratory syncytial virus Parainfluenza virus Influenza A and B. Mycoplasma pneumoniae Adenovirus Coronavirus
What is the most important clinical symptoms?	A barking cough
When does the cough occur?	Suddenly at night
What are other clinical symptoms?	The symptoms can range from mild to life threatening. **Mild**: Normal physical appearance occasional barking cough. **Moderate**: audible stridor agitation, some chest wall retraction with barking cough. **Severe**: frequent barking cough prominent, airway obstruction at rest. Significant agitation, distress lethargy, tachycardia.
Is croup contagious?	Yes, the virus can spread through droplets in the air.
What is the treatment?	Mild symptoms can be managed at home. Dexamethasone can also be given orally. For severe symptoms, the child may require oxygen, nebulized epinephrine, and/or intubation.
What medications should be avoided?	Cough medicine or syrup is not recommended . These may dry and thicken secretions.

Cushing's Syndrome

What is the cause?	A high production of hormones by the adrenal glands. (Glucocorticoids)
What are some major symptoms?	Buffalo hump, moon face, hirsutism lethargy, weakness, and weight gain.
What is the skin of a client with Cushing's syndrome like?	Fragile & bruises easily.

Will this client be overweight?	Yes, weight gain is common.
Will the serum blood glucose levels be high or low?	High. The sodium levels will be increased.
Will the serum potassium levels be high or low?	Low. The calcium levels will be decreased too.
What is the treatment?	Possible hypophysectomy or adrenalectomy then lifelong glucocorticoid therapy.

Cystic Fibrosis

In cystic fibrosis, the _____ _____ _____ or exocrine glands are affected.	Mucus producing glands.
How does cystic fibrosis abnormally change mucus gland secretions?	The mucus will become sticky and cause obstructions.
What are the two systems most affected by cystic fibrosis?	**Respiratory**-the mucus gets trapped in the lungs.
	Digestive- the mucus blocks the pancreas and digestive enzymes, making the absorption of nutrients very difficult.
What is the most accurate test for cystic fibrosis?	Sweat test - the chloride level will be greater than 60 mEq/L.
What are other ways to diagnose cystic fibrosis?	Chest x-ray, stool analysis, and a pulmonary function test.
How does poor absorption of fat in the digestive tract change the appearance of stool?	It causes steatorrhea (greasy, foul--smelling, pale stool)
_____ _____ are given with each meal to help with the absorption of nutrients.	Pancreatic enzymes
What is the most appropriate diet for cystic fibrosis?	High calorie, high protein
_____ _____ is a common technique used to clear thick mucus from the lungs. This is important for preventing respiratory infections.	Postural drainage
What should parents who already have a child with cystic fibrosis do before having another child?	They should get genetic counseling because cystic fibrosis is hereditary.

Data Collection

Type	Objective	Subjective
Definition	Data or information that can be measured	Information the client gives that cannot be measured
How Nurses Obtain It	Observation, Tests, or Measurement	Interviews, Client reports
Examples	Vital signs, Age, Weight, Height	Pain rating, Stress or Anxiety description

Deafness

What are the categories of hearing loss?	According to American National Standards Institute, based on decibels (dB)
	Slight hearing loss: 16-25 dB
	Mild hearing loss: 26-40 dB
	Moderate hearing loss: 41-55 dB
	Severe hearing loss: 71-90 dB
	Profound: more than 90 dB

How is the severity of hearing loss detected?

Aside from the clinical manifestation, a routine audiometry, auditory-evoked brainstem response and otoacoustic emissions hearing tests are used.

What test is used for detecting genetic deafness?

Connexin 26 gene mutation testing.

What is the difference between sensorineural hearing loss and conductive hearing loss?

Sensorineural hearing loss results from an inner ear injury, whereas conductive hearing loss results from a breakdown or obstruction in the outer sand/or middle ear.

True or False: Conductive hearing loss can be treated medically.

True. It is caused by infection such as otitis media, it can be treated by antibiotics. Obstructing cerumen can also be removed.

Managing sensorineural hearing loss is initiated with use of _____.

Hearing aids. It amplifies sound allowing the client to hear. Sensorineural hearing loss cannot be treated medically.

What is cochlear implantation?

A surgical procedure that uses cochlear implant to deliver sound impulses to the hearing (auditory) nerve bypassing damaged sections of the ear.

True or False: Smartphones are also used as a means of communication for hard hearing clients.

True. Smartphones can be communication boards.

This is the most common communication method which uses hand gestures and movements, body language, and facial expressions to communicate to clients with hearing loss.

Sign language.

What is a sign language without the visual effects?

Tactile sign language is a method used by those who are unable to see sign language. To receive the message, the client will lay one or two hands on top of signer's hands.

Deep Vein Thrombosis

What is a deep vein thrombosis (DVT)?

A blood clot in a deep vein that is usually in the leg or calf.

What are the three causes?

Virchow's triad: venous stasis, blood coagulation, vein damage.

What are the risk factors of a DVT?

Immobility, trauma, damage to the vein, pregnancy, surgery.

What blood test is used to detect a DVT?

D-dimer

What are the clinical signs?

Pain, swelling, skin that is warm to the touch.

How is a DVT confirmed?

Venous ultrasound.

What are the 3 types of anticoagulants used to treat a DVT?

Vitamin K, Antagonists
Direct oral anticoagulants
Low molecular weight heparin

What emergency condition can occur if a DVT travels to the lungs?

Pulmonary embolism

What are the nursing interventions?	Measure leg circumference. Apply compression stockings as ordered. Promote hydration. Monitor for bleeding precautions.

Depression

What is depression?	Depression is a mood disorder characterized by a persistent sadness & lack of interest.
Is depression an inherited condition?	It is more common in people who have blood relatives who suffer from it.
Can depression affect a person's daily activities?	A person suffering from depression may have difficulty with routine activities and feel like life is not worth living.
Which transmitters are involved in depression?	Serotonin, dopamine
How do anti-depressants work?	Antidepressants can modify the brain chemistry that causes depression.
What medication is contraindicated with SSRIs?	MAOIs should be avoided because of the side effects and risk of death.

Diabetes Insipidus

What is diabetes insipidus (DI)?	It is usually a pituitary disorder caused by insufficient ADH production. This is called central diabetes insipidus. There's another cause called nephrogenic DI. This happens when the kidneys do not respond to ADH.
What are the causes of diabetes insipidus?	Head injury (common cause) Brain infection/tumor Lithium ingestion (nephrogenic DI)
What are the signs?	Excessive polyuria-no color/odor hypernatremia, nocturia excessive thirst
How is it diagnosed?	Health history, urine & blood test Water deprivation test
What is the treatment?	Hydration and increasing fluids. Intravenous or subcutaneous vasopressin
What are the nursing implications?	Monitoring fluid balance, especially looking for signs of dehydration. Monitor sodium levels. Monitor Intake/output. Low sodium diet

Diabetes Mellitus Type 1

What is diabetes mellitus type 1?	It is a chronic illness in which the pancreas produces little to no insulin.
What is the function of insulin?	Insulin is a hormone that the body utilizes to let sugar (glucose) into cells to convert it into energy.
What causes diabetes mellitus type 1?	An auto-immune disorder

How does the auto-immune response cause diabetes mellitus type 1?

It destroys the pancreatic beta cells which produce insulin.

What are the 3 P's of diabetic symptoms?

Polyphagia (excessive hunger)
Polydipsia (excessive thirst)
Polyuria (excessive urination)

Is there any weight gain?

No weight loss is more common.

Why is infection more common in type 1?

High sugar levels cause the immune system to become weak.

What is tested in hemoglobin A1C?

It is glycosylated hemoglobin testing which determines the average blood sugar level for the previous 3 months.

What are the types of insulin?

See insulin chart in Pharmacology Section.

Diabetes Mellitus Type 2

What is diabetes mellitus type 2?

Type 2 often known as adult-onset diabetes is a disorder caused by a problem with how the body control and uses sugar as energy.

How is type 2 different from type 1?

Type 1 does not make insulin. Type 2 insulin is produced but the body cannot effectively use it.

Is hyperglycemia associated with type 1 or type 2?

Hyperglycemia is a symptom for both.

Can insulin be given as a treatment for type 2?

Type 2 may require insulin therapy. Oral therapy is recommended as well.

How is a fasting blood sugar test performed?

After 8 hours of fasting with nothing to eat except sips of water. Then a blood sample is taken.

How does metformin work?

It works by reducing glucose production in the liver which increases insulin sensitivity allowing the body to use insulin more effectively.

What eye conditions are clients most at risk for?

Glaucoma and cataracts

Diabetic Teaching

Which type of diabetes is controlled mostly by diet and exercise?

Diabetes mellitus type 2

Which type of diabetes is controlled mostly by insulin?

Diabetes mellitus type 1

What should the nurse teach diabetic clients about foot care?

Have the doctor cut the toenails straight across. Inspect the feet daily for sores. Keep the skin clean and dry.

If a diabetic vomits after taking PO anti-diabetic medication what should they do?

Monitor blood sugar; do not repeat dose as medication may have been absorbed.

How often should a diabetic get an eye exam?

Yearly as diabetes can cause retinopathy.

What is insulin lipodystrophy?	It is the result of not rotating SQ insulin injection sites. If the client injects in the same place repeatedly, a fatty mass will appear, decreasing insulin absorption that area. Teach injection site rotation.
Should the client aspirate if injecting insulin SQ?	No.
What is the primary injection site for insulin?	Abdomen
Exercising _____ blood glucose levels.	Lowers
Alcohol, oral contraceptives, aspirin, and MAOIs _____ blood glucose.	Lower
Infection, dehydration, stress, and surgery _____ blood glucose levels.	Increase
What should the nurse give to the client who is hypoglycemic and UNCONSCIOUS?	Glucagon (IV or IM)
Insulin pumps that are wearable mimic which organ?	Pancreas
What is the insulin used in the wearable insulin pump?	Regular or short-acting
How often is the insertion site changed when a client wears an insulin pump?	Every 2 to 3 days
Is the insulin delivered continuous or intermittently?	Continuous
What should clients be advised not to do while wearing an insulin pump?	Smoke cigarettes or drink alcohol.

Dialysis

What are the 2 types of dialysis?	1. Hemodialysis 2. Peritoneal dialysis (PD)
What is the purpose of hemodialysis?	It removes nitrogenous waste products, excess fluid and electrolytes from the blood by means of an artificial kidney.
What are the two types of hemodialysis accesses available to clients?	Grafts and shunts
Which one lasts longer a graft or shunt?	AV shunts/fistulas
Which one is prone to blood clots a graft or a shunt?	AV grafts
Which one is MORE prone to infection a graft or a shunt?	A graft requires more frequent monitoring.
What are the clinical sign of infection of the hemodialysis access?	Redness, swelling, and drainage.
How long does hemodialysis take to complete?	3-5 hours.
What is the purpose of peritoneal dialysis?	It removes nitrogenous waste products, excess fluid and electrolytes from the blood by means of the peritoneal membrane.

Hemodialysis Access	Grafts	Shunts	Central Venous Catheter
What is the purpose?	To connect the client's bloodstream to the dialysis machine.	To connect the client's bloodstream to the dialysis machine.	An emergency access site for immediate dialysis
What is it?	A synthetic tube that is surgically placed under the skin, connecting an *artery* to a *vein*. Will be written as "AV graft"	Also known as a *fistula*, a surgical connection of an *artery* and a *vein* in the arm creating a natural access site. *It is made of the client's own tissue. Will be written as "AV fistula"	A flexible long tube that is threaded through the skin into a central vein in the neck, chest, or groin.
How soon can it be used for dialysis?	3-6 weeks	1 to 4 months	Immediate use
How long does it last?	Approximately 2-3 years	Gold Standard 10 years or more	Should be removed quickly. May damage central veins.
Nursing interventions	This is best if a client has blocked or damaged veins. Requires needles to access the graft. Fistulas are more likely to be useable when they meet the rule of 6's -Flow greater than -600 mL/min -Diameter at least 0.6 -No more than 0.6 cm deep. Nurses and clients should wear a surgical mask during connect and disconnect procedures. Nurses should wear gloves.	Listen for the sound of blood flowing through the AV fistula. This is called a "bruit" and indicates the AV fistula is working. Also, a vibration can be felt on the overlying skin, this is referred to as a "thrill." This is also an indication of proper function. This access may require another type of temporary access during the healing and maturation phase. Needles are required to access the AV fistula for hemodialysis. Nurses and clients should wear a surgical mask during connect and disconnect procedures. Nurses should wear gloves.	Teach the client this type of access can increase the length of hemodialysis treatment. Heparin is used to maintain permeability. Complications of frequent heparin administration are alopecia, allergic reactions, thrombocytopenia, and bleeding. Nurses and Clients should wear a surgical mask during connect and disconnect procedures. Nurses should wear gloves.

Peritoneal dialysis access	PD catheter
What is the purpose?	A catheter which uses the lining of the abdomen (peritoneum) and a dialysate solution to clean the blood.
What is it?	A flexible hollow tube about the size of a straw that is surgically placed in the abdomen.
How soon can it be used for dialysis?	Although it can be used immediately it is best to wait 10-14 days for the catheter site to heal.
How long does it last?	Many years
Nursing interventions?	Teach clients to practice good hand hygiene. Clients should avoid clothing that is too tight. Access sites should be inspected daily for signs of infection. Teach the client that the solution will have to stay in the abdomen for 4 to 6 hours. This is called the "dwell time."

What are the advantages of PD?

Dialysis can be performed at home. It takes less time to finish. Clients should wear a mask when accessing port site.

Does blood leave the body with PD?

No, client's blood does not leave the body.

During the client's dwell time can they move around?

Yes, the client is free to move around and go about their normal activities.

How long does dwell time last?

It can be 4-6 hours. The exchange of solution is 30-40 minutes.

What is the name of the infection that can develop in the abdomen as a result of PD?

Peritonitis

What are the clinical signs of peritonitis?

1. A swollen/distended abdomen.
2. Pain and tenderness in abdomen.
3. Dialysis drain fluid that is cloudy.
4. An exit site that is red and has pus.
5. Fever, nausea, and vomiting.

How is peritonitis treated?

Antibiotics, it is possible for the antibiotics to be put inside of the dialysate solution.

Digestive System

What is another name for the digestive system?	Alimentary canal
What is the entry point of the alimentary canal?	The mouth
Which division of the nervous system is responsible for digestive system control?	Parasympathetic nervous system
In the duodenum what is neutralized in pancreatic secretions?	Chyme
What do liver enzymes convert ammonia into?	Urea
Which vitamin is absorbed through the large intestine?	Vitamin K
Through which body part is solid waste expelled?	Anus
What are the major hormones produced by the stomach?	Gastrin, ghrelin
What are parietal cells?	Cells in the stomach that produce acid.
What are the major hormones produced by pancreas?	Secretin, somatostatin, insulin, glucagon
What are the major hormones produced by the small intestine?	Cholecystokinin, secretin somatostatin, motilin

Diverticulitis

What is diverticulitis?	A painful form of inflammation in the digestive tract.
What are the accompanying symptoms?	Left lower abdominal pain hyperthermia change in bowel habits.
What are the risk factors?	A red meat diet, obesity, smoking Alcohol use, NSAIDS
How is diverticulitis diagnosed?	Blood tests, stool sample, digital rectal exam, colonoscopy.
What is the treatment?	Antibiotics - Encourage a diet high in fiber. Clients may be NPO or clear liquid diet.

Domestic Violence

What are signs of domestic violence in children?	Frequent bruises or burns, shrinking back when an adult approaches & hitting others.
What two factors play an important part in domestic violence?	Power and control, as the abuser sees the victim as a possession.
What are the various types of abuse?	Physical, verbal, emotional, sexual and financial.
What are signs of neglect in children?	Stealing food, lack of dental care, poor hygiene, poor school attendance, saying that no one is home.
When a victim of rape shows no emotion or feelings after an attack, what is this called?	Controlled pattern response.

 Study more at ReMarNurse.com | Join live weekly on YouTube @ReMarNurse

What are the 5 stages of domestic violence in an intimate relationship?

Honeymoon stage, buildup of stress, anger, beating, and then reconciliation.

Should a rape victim take a shower before coming to the hospital for treatment?

No physical evidence may be washed away in the shower.

If a client comes into the hospital afraid for their life due to domestic abuse, should the nurse suggest they do not return home?

Yes, the nurse should help the client explore other housing options.

What is sexual abuse by a family member called?

Incest.

Donning Sterile Gloves

Gather all of the necessary supplies.
Wash and dry hands.
Place package on a dry waist-high surface.
Open package using outer one-inch margin, facing gloves toward you.
With two fingers on the non-dominant hand, pick up cuff of first glove.
Place glove on dominant hand.
Slide gloved fingers into the cuff of the other sterile glove.
Place the non-dominant hand into the glove, making sure not to touch the outside of the glove.
With both hands gloved, touch only the sterile area to adjust the gloves for comfort.

Drug Allergies

Allergy	Patient Response	Nursing Interventions
Anaphylactic reaction	Rash, hives, difficulty breathing, increased BP, dilated pupils, tachycardia. This reaction is immediate. Swelling of the mucous membranes and constricting bronchi can lead to respiratory arrest.	Administer epinephrine 0.3 mL subcutaneously. Massage the site to speed absorption rate.
Cytotoxic reaction	Antibodies circulate in the blood and attack the blood cells. The patient will have (decreased hematocrit, WBCs, and platelets). The liver enzymes will also be elevated.	Notify the healthcare provider and discontinue the drug. Await intervention orders.
Delayed allergic reaction	Occurs several hours to days after exposure. Rash, hives, swollen joints. This is more similar to skin irritation or poison ivy.	Notify the healthcare provider. Provide skin care and continue comfort measures. Topical corticosteroids may be prescribed.

Dysmenorrhea Chart

Definition	Cause	Symptoms	Management
Dysmenorrhea is characterized by painful abdominal cramps during menstruation.	Primary dysmenorrhea develops by prostaglandins, hormone-like chemicals in the uterus that induce the uterine muscle to contract. Prostaglandins are also involved in the excessive bleeding that occurs with dysmenorrhea. A variety of medical problems can cause secondary dysmenorrhea, including: -Endometriosis -Uterine fibroids -Pelvic inflammatory disease -Ovarian cysts -Ectopic pregnancy -Intrauterine device use.	Sharp or painful cramping in the lower abdomen, which can be strong. Pain radiates in the lower back and thighs and begins 1 to 3 days before the period starts, peaks 24 hours after it begins, and subsides in 2 to 3 days. A dull, constant discomfort. Some females also have: -Nausea -Loose bowel -Headache -Dizziness	To relieve menstrual cramps, the doctor may prescribe: Pain relievers. Over-the-counter pain medicines can help control cramp pain. Nonsteroidal anti-inflammatory medications (NSAIDs) are also available on prescription. Hormonal contraception. Oral contraceptives contain hormones that inhibit ovulation and lessen the severity of menstrual cramps. Surgery. If the cramps are caused by a condition such as endometriosis or fibroids, surgery to repair the problem could reduce the symptoms.

Ebola Virus Disease

What is the ebola virus?

It is a fatal hemorrhagic fever.

How is it transmitted?

Through direct contact.

What is the average incubation period?

8-10 days.

What are the clinical signs?

Fever, severe headache, muscle pain, weakness diarrhea, vomiting, stomach pain, unexplained bleeding.

What is the isolation precaution required?

Contact precautions

What is the treatment?

Providing fluids/ electrolytes offering oxygen therapy. Isolation to a private room. Monitor for bleeding. Watch for shock.

Eczema

What is eczema?

Also known as atopic dermatitis. The condition is a long-term skin rash.

What can trigger eczema?

Stress, changes in temperatures, skin infections, dust mites, molds, food allergies.

What are the clinical symptoms?

A dry, itchy, red, scaly rash. The rash can be oozing and crusty. It can start on the face and spread to the neck scalp, hands, arms, and feet. It can be found in the folds of the skin.

What is the client education for eczema?

Avoid scratching. Keep the skin moisturized. Wear light cotton clothes and avoid wool. Use a humidifier in the home to keep the air moist.

Endocrine System

Which other system does the endocrine system pair with to send signals?

Nervous System

Are hormones chemical or electrical messengers?

Chemical

Which organ is responsible for insulin production?

Pancreas

Which gland is responsible for absorbing calcium in the body?

Parathyroid gland

List the hormone that induces ovulation?

Luteinizing

List the non-polar fat soluble hormones:

Estrogen & Progestogen

List a polar water-soluble hormone:

Epinephrine, norepinephrine, calcitonin, melatonin

What metabolic disease is caused by insufficient insulin production?

Diabetes mellitus

Will a diabetic patient have a blood sugar level that is too high or too low?

Too high

What metabolic condition is caused by an increased production of the thyroid hormone?

Hyperthyroidism

What is gigantism?	Rare abnormal growth condition in children.
Gigantism occurs when there is a tumor in what location?	Pituitary gland
What lymphoid organ produces T-cells?	Thymus
Which hormone stimulates interstitial cells of the testes?	Luteinizing
What is the loss of water concentration in the blood?	Dehydration
What is the pituitary gland also called?	The master gland
When is melatonin production at its highest?	During the night to promote sleep.

Endometriosis

What is endometriosis?	A disorder in which tissue grows outside of the uterus in places it should not be.
What causes the condition?	There are many theories. Most are problems with menstrual period flow.
What are the common symptoms?	Painful periods, cramping, bleeding infertility, painful sexual intercourse, fatigue, and anxiety.
How is it prevented?	Through early detection and management.
How is it diagnosed?	Ultrasound, MRI, histological verification.
What is the treatment?	Non-steroidal anti-inflammatory drugs, analgesics, hormonal medicine, laparoscopic surgery.

Epiglottitis

What is epiglottis and what does it do?	It is a flap of skin at the base of the tongue. It opens and closes during breathing.
What is the cause of epiglottitis?	Haemophilus influenzae
Is this caused by a virus or bacteria?	Bacteria
What is the usual age of children who get epiglottitis	2 - 5 years old
What are the signs of epiglottitis?	4 D's (Drooling, Dysphagia, Dysphonia [no voice] and Distress).
What will the child look like during an episode of epiglottitis?	Sitting upright, drooling shallow, rapid, breathing, a protruding tongue is seen.
Can epiglottitis be treated at home?	No, the child must go to the hospital immediately.
When assessing the airway should a tongue depressor or tongue blade be used?	NO, NEVER put anything in the mouth to assess!
If the child cannot breathe, what might be done?	Intubation
Which medication will be given to treat epiglottitis?	Antibiotic therapy
How can epiglottitis be avoided?	By getting the H. influenza vaccine

Epilepsy

What is epilepsy?	Recurrent seizures, short uncontrolled movements that may affect the entire body (generalized) or only some parts (partial).
How are seizures classified?	Seizures are divided into different types according to where they begin in the brain, the movements noted, the length of time of the seizure.
What are the psychological symptoms?	Fear, anxiety, and sense of Déjà vu.
How does anti-epileptic medications work?	Anti-epileptic drugs function by modifying the chemicals in the brain.
What are the common side effects of the medication?	Drowsiness, lack of energy, nervousness, headaches, tremors, hair loss, uncontrollable trembling swollen gums.,
What drug reaction requires immediate medical attention?	Rashes- may indicate a significant adverse drug reaction in the client.

Epistaxis

What is epistaxis?	"Epistaxis" is the medical terminology for nosebleeds. A nosebleed, defined as the loss of blood from the tissue lining the nose, can happen in either one or both nostrils.
What are the types of epistaxis?	**Anterior nosebleed** - begins at the front of the nose. This is the most common type of epistaxis, usually not serious and can be managed at home.
	Posterior nosebleed - happens deep within the nose. Larger blood vessels are affected, resulting in severe bleeding that may extend to the back of the throat. It requires rapid medical intervention and is more common in adults.
What causes epistaxis?	Dry air is the most common cause of epistaxis. Dry air is caused by hot, low-humidity areas or heated interior air. Both conditions cause the nasal membrane (the fragile tissue inside the nose) to dry up and crack. This increases the likelihood of bleeding when rubbed, picked, or blown through the nostrils.
Why do high altitudes cause epistaxis?	Nasal blood vessels can expand and constrict due to altitude and air pressure changes. Disruptions can cause nosebleeds.
What is the first aid for epistaxis at home?	Maintain the head up. Lean forward to keep the blood from going down the throat. Pinch the nose for 10-15 mins to apply pressure on the blood arteries, which helps to stop blood flow. Applying an ice pack to the nose's bridge will help constrict blood vessels further, lessen bleeding, and promote comfort.

Is a humidifier useful in preventing epistaxis?	Adding a humidifier to the furnace or running a humidifier in the bedroom at night provides moisture to the air.
Is drinking allowed after epistaxis?	Yes, it is important to drink enough water following a nosebleed. Water, juice, and other non-caffeinated drinks are all good choices. Some blood may leak down the back to the throat into the stomach during epistaxis. This may result in an unpleasant taste or nausea. However, drinking water will not affect this.

Erectile Dysfunction

What hormone is increased in erectile dysfunction (ED)?	Luteinizing hormone.
What is the natural cause of ED?	Age
What are the unnatural causes of ED?	Cardiovascular disease, DM, hypertension, obesity, smoking, depression.
What is the drug of choice for ED?	Avanafil, sildenafil, tadalafil. These medications relax muscles and increases blood flow.
Which medication should not be taken when taking treatment for ED?	Nitroglycerin can cause severe hypotension.

Fibromyalgia

What are the clinical signs?	Generalized pain, fatigue, sleep disturbance that lasts for 3 months without cause.
How is fibromyalgia diagnosed?	A physical examination, pain history, and diagnostic tests.
Is there a cure for fibromyalgia?	No there is no cure.
What is the treatment?	Stress management NSAIDS, muscle relaxants. The goal is to improve the quality of the client's life.

Fractures Chart

What is a bone fracture?	Bone fracture occurs when a force exerted against a bone is stronger than the bone can bear.
How many weeks does it take to heal a bone fracture?	3 to 12 weeks. It depends on age and health status of the patient.
What are the signs of a bone fracture?	Remember the BROKEN! **B**ruising all around the area and pain. **R**educed mobility of the muscle or extremity. **O**dd appearance. **Kr**akling sounds from fragments rubbing (crepitus). **E**rythema and edema at the location. **N**eurovascular dysfunction.

What are the 6 P's of neurovascular impairment?	1. Pain 2. Pallor 3. Paralysis 4. Paresthesia 5. Poikilothermia 6. Pulselessness (late sign)
What is Compound vs Simple fracture?	**Compound (open) fracture** - a fractured bone that breaks through the skin. **Simple (closed) fracture** - a fractured bone that does not penetrate through the skin.
What is a Complete vs Incomplete fracture?	**Complete fracture** - the fracture completely separates the bone in two. **Incomplete fracture** - the fracture does not break the bone all the way through.
What is Greenstick vs Comminuted?	**Greenstick** - one side of the bone is bent while the other is broken. incomplete type of fracture. **Comminuted** - the bone is broken into many fragments (3 or more).
What is Transverse vs Oblique?	**Transverse** – the fracture is straight across the bone shaft. **Oblique** - the fracture is slanted across the bone shaft.
What is spiral fracture?	**Spiral**: the fracture twists around the bone (from twisting injury).
What is compartment syndrome?	This can occur when there is bleeding or swelling present after an injury, like with a bone fracture.

Genital Herpes

Which simplex is responsible for genital herpes?	Herpes simplex 2
Which simplex is responsible for oral herpes	Herpes simplex 1
How is genital herpes spread?	During sexual contact or birth.
What are the symptoms for males?	Painful, vesicular lesions
What are the symptoms for females?	Painful, vesicular lesions
Are these lesions always present on the body?	No, they come and go.
If lesions are present in a pregnant woman, how should she deliver?	C-section
What triggers outbreaks of genital herpes?	Stress, anxiety, sunlight fatigue, and illness.
How often should a woman with herpes get a pap smear?	Every six months.
Can genital herpes be cured?	No cure.
What is the treatment?	Acyclovir

Note the difference between herpes simplex vs. herpes zoster.

Characteristic	Herpes zoster	Herpes simplex
Clinical presentations	Rash in one or two dermatomes, painful and itchy.	Painful vesicular lesions, ulcers, and cold sores.
Pain rating	Severe	Moderate
Skin scaring	Common	No
Lifecycle	Lives in a client forever once infected.	Lives in a client forever once infected.
Treatment	Vaccine, oral antivirals, local anesthetics, NSAIDS, nerve pain medication.	Vaccine, oral antivirals, local anesthetics, NSAIDS, nerve pain medication.
Vaccine	Vaccine available for both primary infection and shingles.	Vaccine available for both primary infection and shingles.

Reaching your goals is not about working all day without a break.
It is about being intentional with your time and where you spend it.

Genitourinary System

What is another name for the genitourinary system (GU)?
Urogenital

What structure takes urine to the urinary bladder after it is produced by the kidneys?
Ureters

What structure can carry urine and sperm?
Urethra

Which vitamin can the kidneys produce?
Vitamin D

What is the functional unit of the kidney called?
Nephron

What is the job of the nephron?
Filtering urine & excretion

What are the two major regions of the kidneys?
Cortex & Medulla

Where is the glomerulus of the nephron located?
In the renal cortex
(outer layer-kidney)

What happens in the renal cortex?
Blood is filtered

What happens in the renal medulla?
Salt and water are reabsorbed to make urine.

What kind of ducts are urine released to?
Collecting ducts

Where do collecting ducts drain?
Into a renal pelvis

What waste products do urine contain?
Urea, water, salts & excess metabolites

The kidneys work with the heart to control
_____ _____ .
Blood pressure

The heart pumps blood to the kidneys via which artery?
Renal artery

The renal vein brings what to the blood?
Vital nutrients

The kidneys produce what hormone to regulate blood pressure by removing or retaining salt and water?
Renin

How many ureters are present?
2

What structure holds urine until it is excreted?
Urinary bladder

The urinary bladder has sensors to communicate with what system?
Central nervous system

What must relax in the urinary bladder for excretion to occur?
Internal & external sphincters

Gestational Diabetes

What is the cause of gestational diabetes?

Gestational diabetes is caused by hormonal changes during pregnancy that affects insulin sensitivity.

What are the risk factors?

Maternal age over 25, clients who are obese and who have been pregnant multiple times.

At what point in pregnancy does it begin?

Second to third trimester.

Does it go away after delivery?

Yes, the condition should resolve itself and blood glucose levels should return to normal.

What are the clinical symptoms?

Increased hunger and thirst, frequent urination, Recurrent infections, dry mouth and itchy skin. However usually the patient cannot distinguish the signs, which is why every pregnant woman is screened.

Is exercise recommended during pregnancy?

Regular physical activity is important in maintaining a healthy blood glucose level during pregnancy.

How is gestational diabetes treated?

Mother: Daily blood sugar monitoring, healthy diet, and exercise.
Fetus: a non-stress test may be ordered.

Which antidiabetic medication is safe to give?

Insulin is the first line choice. Metformin is also safe to administer. Glyburide is also safe to administer.

What is macrosomia?

It is the term for a newborn with a larger than average weight.

What are the nursing considerations for macrosomia?

This infant has an increased for injuries during birth. For example, shoulder dystocia, bone fractures and brachial plexus injury.

The infant with macrosomia is at a high risk for?

Hypoglycemia, Jaundice, Respiratory distress *These babies are big but they require extra health monitoring.

What are the clinical signs of newborn hypoglycemia?

Jitteriness, apnea, cyanosis and tachypnea.

What is the treatment for newborn hypoglycemia?

Oral milk feedings are the initial intervention. Buccal dextrose gel can also be given when the symptoms are mild. In severe cases IV dextrose is administered.

Glasgow Coma Scale

What is Glasgow coma scale?

It is a tool to "score" or measure how conscious a patient is.

What are the 3 parameters of GCS?

EMV
Eye response (E)
Verbal response (V)
Motor response (M)

What are the 3 requirements of consciousness?

Awake, alert, oriented.

When will the nurse know that the client is in a coma state?

Score: 3 to 8
No eye opening, no ability to follow commands, no word verbalizations.

In head injury classification, if the GCS is 8 or less, what does it mean?

Severe head injury.

In head injury classification, if the GCS is 9-12 what does it mean?

Moderate hard injury.

In head injury classification, if the GCS is 13-15 What does it mean?

Mild head injury.

What is the lowest score for GCS? 1-15

3.

In GCS-P, What "P" stands for?

Pupil.

Glaucoma

How does glaucoma affect vision?

It becomes blurry and the client experiences tunnel vision. There will also be halos around the light.

This condition can be acute or chronic due to ____ ____ ____.

Increased intraocular pressure.

_____ is the simple, painless procedure Used to measure intraocular pressure.

Tonometry.

What are the two types of glaucoma?

Open angle and closed angle

Which one is painful?

Closed angle is painful but it is not the most common of the two types.

State the class of drug used to constrict the pupil and let aqueous hum.

Miotics

Give an example of a miotic medication?

Timolol or pilocarpine

Why might diuretics be given to clients with glaucoma?

To decrease aqueous humor production.

Which diuretic is usually prescribed?

Osmitrol because it dehydrates or draws water out of the vitreous humor.

Never give _____ because they dilate the pupils.

Mydriatics

If surgery is required, what should be monitored for post-operatively?

Hemorrhage

What post-op teaching should be done?

No straining, heavy lifting, crying, or rubbing the eyes.

Glomerulonephritis

What is glomerulonephritis?	It is an inflammation of the filters in the kidneys (glomeruli).
Is it fluid overload or a fluid deficit?	It is an issue that results in fluid overload.
What are the signs of fluid overload?	Bounding and increased pulse, distended hand and neck veins, elevated CVP, and dysrhythmias.
What are the two types of glomerulonephritis?	**Acute:** This occurs 2 to 3 weeks after a streptococcal infection. **Chronic:** This may occur after the acute phase or slowly over time.
What are the medical complications associated with glomerulonephritis?	Kidney failure, hypertensive, encephalopathy, pulmonary edema heart failure.
What type of edema will be seen every morning?	Periorbital and facial edema.
Will the urinary output decrease or increase?	Decreased urinary output.
What is the most effective measure to determine the fluid balance?	Measuring the daily weight.
Will the BUN and creatinine levels be high or low?	Increased blood urea nitrogen and creatinine levels.
What are the clinical signs of glomerulonephritis?	Gross hematuria, dark, cola colored or brown colored urine.

Gout

What is gout?	It is an inflammatory arthritis that makes the joints painful swollen.
What causes gout?	When uric acid levels rise in the body, gout develops and produces needle-like urate crystals in a joint or surrounding tissue, causing pain and inflammation.
What triggers a gout attack?	Conditions that increase the body's temperature, excessive alcohol consumption, eating fatty meals, dehydration, and joint injury.
What food has high purine content?	Red and organ meat, seafood including: anchovies, sardines, mussels, scallops, trout, and tuna.
Is it okay to put a cold compress on the swollen joint?	Yes, it is ok to apply a cold compress or ice pack to the affected joint for 15-20 minutes several times daily.
Can gout be inherited?	The genetic background of gout is unknown. However, having a close relative with gout increases a person's risk of developing the condition.

 Study more at ReMarNurse.com | Join live weekly on YouTube @ReMarNurse

Guillain-Barre Syndrome

What system is affected by Guillain-Barre syndrome?	Peripheral nervous system (PNS).
How does Guillain-Barre syndrome affect the PNS?	Guillain-Barre syndrome (GBS) is a neurological condition in which the immune system mistakenly attacks a portion of the peripheral nervous system.
What causes Guillain-Barre syndrome?	The exact cause remains unknown. However, the condition is frequently associated with a viral or bacterial infection.
Which infection is related to developing GBS?	Campylobacter bacteria, flu virus, cytomegalovirus, HIV, dengue virus, zika, Epstein-Barr virus, hepatitis A, B, C, and E. Mycoplasma pneumonia, Covid-19.
What are the common symptoms of GBS?	Tingling and weakens in the feet and legs that spread to the upper body and arms. However, it can also start in the arms or face. Muscle weakness might progress to paralysis as the condition advances.
Is there any test to diagnose GBS?	GBS may be hard to identify in its early stages, although the following tests can be used: Spinal tap, electromyography, and nerve conduction study.
Is there any treatment for GBS?	There is no treatment for GBS. However, two procedures may promote recovery and minimize its severity: plasma exchange and immunoglobulin therapy.

Hand Foot & Mouth Disease

What is it caused by?	Coxsackievirus A16.
How is HFMD transmitted?	It is transmitted from person to person through fecal oral route or via contact with skin lesions and oral secretions.
What are the clinical signs?	The virus causes sores in the mouth and a rash on the hands and feet, fever, sore throat, & loss of appetite are common.
How long do the symptoms last?	The virus clears up on its own in 10 days.
What isolation precaution is required?	Contact precautions

Hand Hygiene

What is hand hygiene?	It is a general term that applies to handwashing, antiseptic handwash, antiseptic hand rub, or surgical antisepsis.
What are the 5 moment of hand hygiene?	1. Before touching a client. 2. Before a clean/aseptic procedure. 3. After a body fluid exposure risk. 4. After touching a client. 5. After touching client's surroundings.

The nurse does not need to worry about washing hands if gloves are worn during client care. True or False?	False, the use of gloves does not replace the need for cleaning the hands.
What is the duration of the entire procedure during handwashing?	At least 20 seconds
What is hand rub?	It is a gel or liquid containing antimicrobial agents that decrease the number of microorganisms present on the hands. The antimicrobial agents in most hand rubs are alcohols (ethanol, isopropanol, n-propanol) available in varying concentrations.
What is the duration of the entire procedure during rubbing?	20 to 30 seconds.
What is the sterile technique that prevents contamination of open wound, serves to isolate the operative area from the unsterile environment, and maintains a sterile field for surgery?	Surgical asepsis.
What is known as clean technique which includes procedures used to reduce the number of organisms on the hands?	Medical asepsis.
What is often acquired during direct contact with clients or contaminated surfaces. It colonizes superficial layers of the skin. It is most frequently associated with healthcare-associated infections?	Transient flora.
What is attached to deeper layers of the skin. It is more resistant to removal and less likely to be associated with health-care associated infections?	Resident flora.

Heart Failure

What is heart failure?	A progressive condition in which heart's muscle is injured. The heart loses its ability to pump enough to meet the body's needs.
What are the risk factors of heart failure?	Aging, HTN, MI, coronary artery disease, congenital heart disease diabetes, obesity.
What are the clinical symptoms?	Dyspnea, orthopnea, paroxysmal nocturnal dyspnea, exercise intolerance edema, ascites.
How is heart failure diagnosed?	Echocardiogram, EKG, stress test, a complete blood count.
How is heart failure treated?	ACE inhibitors, beta blockers cardiac glycosides, nitrates, diuretics
What are the surgical treatments?	Heart transplant, defibrillator placement

Hemophilia

What is the common type?

Factor VIII and IX deficiency.

What is the risk factor of having this condition?

Genetics

What are the clinical findings?

Epistaxis, hemarthrosis, a tendency to bruise easily.

What is the primary treatment?

Replacement of the missing clotting factor.

What are the important nursing interventions?

Maintain bleeding precautions.
Monitor for any pain.
Assess neurological status.
Instruct the client to wear protective devices such as helmets or knee pads.

Hepatitis

What is hepatitis?

It is a serious inflammation of the liver.

What are the different kinds of hepatitis?

Infectious hepatitis has six types:
A, B, C, D, E, G.
The non-infectious types are autoimmune & alcoholic hepatitis.

How is hepatitis transmitted?

See chart below.

Hepatitis A	Exposure of virus in food or water
Hepatitis B	Exposure of the virus in body fluids such as blood, vaginal secretions, or semen.
Hepatitis C	Exposure to virus in body fluids such as blood, vaginal secretions, or semen.
Hepatitis D	Exposure to blood containing the virus.
Hepatitis E	Exposure to the virus in food or water.

Can hepatitis be passed down or inherited?

Hepatitis cannot be genetically inherited but it can be passed down from a mother to a newborn during the birthing process.

What are the general clinical signs of hepatitis?

Low grade fever, abdominal pain, bloating, fatigue, nausea vomiting, itching, loss of appetite, jaundice.

What is jaundice?

It is a yellowing of the skin, whites of the eyes, and mucous membranes. This is caused by a buildup of bilirubin in the blood. No, not everyone who

Do all types of hepatitis?

is infected may have symptoms such as jaundice. Adults experience hepatitis symptoms more frequently than children.

Are vaccinations available for all kinds of hepatitis?

There are only vaccines available for hepatitis A & B.

What is the treatment for hepatitis?

The treatment for hepatitis depends on the type. Viral hepatitis C & D may be treated with an antiviral medication. Hepatitis A, B, E often clears up on its own. Autoimmune hepatitis can be controlled with drugs that suppress the immune system. Alcoholic hepatitis treatment involves nutritional support.

Is hepatitis preventable?

Vaccination can prevent some types of infections. Avoiding alcohol or drinking in moderation is the best approach to prevent alcoholic hepatitis. Most cases of autoimmune hepatitis cannot be avoided. Understanding the risk factors helps in early detection and treatment of the condition.

Human Papillomavirus

What is human papillomavirus (HPV)?

HPV infection is a viral infection that causes skin or mucus membrane growths.

Is HPV a sexually transmitted infection?

Yes. This is spread through direct skin to skin contact.

How can this condition be prevented?

Through vaccination, safe sex use of condom.

Who should get the HPV vaccine?

Teenage girls and boys up to age 26

What are the clinical findings?

Warts, unusual growths, lumps, and sores.

What is the treatment?

The virus cannot be treated. However, the warts caused by the virus can be removed through the following: cryosurgery, electrocautery, laser therapy.

Hyperbilirubinemia

What is considered an elevated serum bilirubin level?

Serum levels higher than 12mg/dl.

What are the clinical signs of this condition?

The condition presents with excess bilirubin in the bloodstream. Dark colored urine. Pale clay colored stool can also be present if the liver is the source of the issue.

What will a newborn's skin look like?

Jaundice —a yellow pigment usually seen on first day of life. Adults will also present with yellowing of the skin and sclera.

Why does the skin and sclera turn yellow?

Because bilirubin is yellow.

What is bilirubin?

Bilirubin is the yellow substance the body creates when red blood cells break down.

What is the treatment for increased bilirubin levels?

Phototherapy for newborns. Breastfeeding or increased feedings should also be encouraged. With adults jaundice usually isn't treated the focus is on the condition causing the jaundice. Once that condition is treated the jaundice will go away.

Hyperthyroidism

What are the primary hormones that the thyroid produces?

Triiodothyronine (T3) and thyroxine (T4).

What is the most common cause of hyperthyroidism?

Grave's disease.

Does hyperthyroidism cause weight loss?

When the thyroid gland produces too many hormones its rate of metabolism increases. This implies that body will begin to burn more calories than it requires. This can result in weight loss.

What eye complication does hyperthyroidism cause?

Grave's ophthalmopathy is a condition that develops in persons who have grave's disease, which causes an overactive thyroid. Exophthalmos may be seen.

Is it cold intolerance or heat intolerance for hyperthyroidism?

The thyroid gland maintains the body temperature rises. When the thyroid gland produces more hormones than the body requires. As a result, the client is extremely sensitive to heat and perspires constantly.

What food to avoid?

In some situations, eating too many iodine-rich or iodine-fortified food might develop or worsen hyperthyroidism.

What is the most appropriate nursing action before a thyroid function tests?

Determine if the client is allergic to iodine (shellfish). Or has consumed medications or agents containing iodine during thyroid exams, which may affect the test results.

Hypothyroidism

What is the function of the thyroid gland?

The thyroid gland produces T3 and T4 hormone that regulates metabolism, body temperature, and heart rate.

What is the difference between hyper & hypo?

The difference is the amount of thyroid hormone that is produced and released.

What autoimmune disorder can lead to hypothyroidism?

Hashimoto's disease.

What do high TSH and low T4 levels suggest?

High TSH and low T4 levels in the blood may indicate an underactive thyroid.

What does high TSH and normal T4 levels suggest?

If the TSH levels are elevated but the T4 levels are normal this may also indicate an underactive thyroid especially in the future.

Does hypothyroidism cause cold intolerance?

Yes, clients will experience cold intolerance because they don't produce adequate thyroid hormone to effectively convert and utilize stored energy.

What are other signs of a hypoactive thyroid?

Fatigue, weight gain, muscle pain, dry skin, heavy/irregular, menstrual cycle, depression, bradycardia.

What is the medical emergency involved with hypothyroidism?	Myxedema is a life threatening event It involves the swelling of the skin and underlying tissues. It can also be called a myxedema coma.
How will the mental status of the client be?	It will rapidly deteriorate.
In the myxedema will the edema be pitting?	The swelling will be a non-pitting edema.
List other symptoms of myxedema:	Macroglossia, ptosis, periorbital edema, goiter, thin coarse hair, hypothermia.
What is the treatment of myxedema?	ICU placement, replacement of steroid hormone, mechanical ventilation may be necessary.

Huntington's Disease

What kind of disease is this?	It is an inherited disorder in which the nerve cells in the brain breakdown.
Which organ is most affected?	The brain because neurons die which control various body movements.
What are symptoms of the disease?	Uncontrolled movement called chorea, and behavioral changes. Muscle rigidity is noted. Impaired gait. Impaired judgement and cognition also are common.
What age is most affected?	30 to 50 years old.
Is there a cure?	No, the disease will get progressively worse.

Immune System

What is a blood protein that fights against a specific antigen?	Antibody
What is an antigen?	Substance on the surface of agents that act to identify them.
What are the diverse set of microbial patterns that alert immune cells to destroy pathogens?	Pathogen Associated Molecular Patterns
Where do B cells originate?	Bone marrow
Where do T cells mature?	Thymus gland
Skin and mucous membranes are examples of what kind of barriers?	External barriers
What are phagocytes?	Cells that engulf & absorb foreign cells.
Which kind of antigen presenting cells present processed antigen material to T-cells?	Dendritic cell
What is an interferon?	A protein released by a host cell in the presence of viruses, bacteria, tumors to signal an immune response.

What is a leukocyte?	A white blood cell (WBC).
What is a monocyte?	The largest WBC.
What are NK cells?	These "natural killer" cells are another type of lymphocyte.
Are NK cells innate or adaptive?	Innate
What is an immunoglobulin?	Any protein that functions as an antibody.
What are the two types of lymphocytes?	T cells and b cells.
Which lymphocytes oversees humoral immunity?	B cells
What is phagocytosis?	The process of cell ingestion.
What are the four types of phagocytes or white blood cells?	1. Macrophages 2. dendritic cells 3. neutrophils 4. eosinophils
What is a lysozyme?	An enzyme that can break down a bacterial cell wall.
CD4 cells are also called?	Helper T cells
Hepatitis B rapid treatment is a form of what kind of immunity?	Passive
What kind of medical conditions occur when the body's immune system attacks itself?	Autoimmune
Which virus results in a depressed, underactive immune system?	HIV or AIDS
Which condition is an immune response to the harmless particle pollen?	Allergies
Which condition is an immune response targeted in the lining of the joints causing painful swelling?	Rheumatoid arthritis
Which disabling disease is an immune response that affects the white matter of the brain and spinal cord?	Multiple sclerosis

Immunizations

What vaccine is given at each age?

Birth	Hep B #1
2 months	Hep B #2, DTap, Hib, IPV, PCV
4 months	All 2-month immunizations except Hep B
6 months	All 2-month immunizations
12 months	MMR #1, Hib, PCV, varicella

*some resources say Hep B #2 can be given at 1 month.

Tetanus and diphtheria are optional vaccinations; what is the earliest age they can be give?	2 months.
What is a booster shot?	An additional dose of the vaccination to increase effectiveness.

What are the side effects of vaccines?		Low-grade fever, tenderness, swelling at the site, children may become irritable.
What medication should be given for these effects?		Acetaminophen
Never give ___ to children experiencing these effects.		Aspirin
When should the meningitis vaccination be given?		Before a client goes to college.
If an adult woman receives an MMR shot, what should you teach her?		Wait 3 months before trying to become pregnant. 2 doses of the vaccine should be given 28 days apart.
How soon can a child get the influenza vaccination?		Not until six months.
Do not give MMR or the chickenpox vaccine to clients allergic to what?		Neomycin
What is active immunity?		Stimulating the body to produce antibodies by giving the client a vaccine.
What is passive immunity?		Antibodies that are formed in another body but passed down to another person for short-term use. Examples: When a baby gets their mother's antibodies through the placenta or breast milk.

	Active Immunity	Passive Immunity
How is immunity acquired?	The client has responded to an antigen and produced his/her own antibodies.	The client is given antibodies by someone else.
Types	Natural infection Artificial- induced by vaccines	Natural transfer of maternal antibodies Artificial injection of immunoglobulins
Time Advantage	Immediate immunity	Immunity effective only after lag time.

Impetigo

What is impetigo?		A bacterial infection of the skin that is commonly seen in young children.
What are two bacterias that cause impetigo?		Group A streptococcus and staphylococcus aureus.
What isolation precautions should be taken?		Contact precautions.
How many days does it usually appear?		Sores appear in 10 days after someone is exposed to group A strep bacteria.
When time of year does this usually occur?		The summer is the most frequent time of the year.
What is the most common age range for this to this occur?		2-5 years old.
When applying topical antibiotics, what is most important to teach the client?		Teach the client to remove any crust before applying antibiotic ointment to the lesion.
What area of the body is this commonly seen?		To the exposed skin such as nose, mouth, arms, and legs.
What is the hallmark clinical sign of impetigo?		Yellow crusted over lesions these are honey colored.
When will the client be considered not contagious?		If taking antibiotic ointment: after 24 hours the patient is not contagious.

 Study more at ReMarNurse.com | Join live weekly on YouTube @ReMarNurse

Increased Intracranial Pressure (ICP)

What is the normal intracranial pressure range?	5-15 mm Hg
What are the common causes of ICP?	Trauma, hemorrhage, edema and tumors.
What should the nurse assess?	The level of consciousness (It will decrease as the intracranial pressure increases.)
What is the earliest sign of ICP?	Decreased level of consciousness.
The adult client will often appear?	Restless, agitated, reporting headaches.
What are the signs of ICP in babies?	Bulging fontanelles strabismus, vomiting, seizures, high pitched cry, lethargy.
Client may report ____ ____ ____ ____.	Projectile vomiting without nausea.
How will the vital signs appear with ICP?	Blood pressure (up) Temperature (up) Respiration (up then down) Heart rate (up)
What is widening pulse pressure and how is it related?	When systolic blood pressure goes up and diastolic pressure continues to go down so that they become further apart (e.g. 135/40 is a bad sign!) A widening pulse pressure indicates deteriorating cardiovascular health
What is Cushing's Triad?	Three things: widening pulse pressure, Cheyne stokes respirations, & bradycardia.
Initiate _____ precautions.	Seizure.
What are the late signs of ICP?	Unilateral pupil dilation hypertension, or hypotension bradycardia.
Elevate the head of the bed to?	10 to 30 degrees, to promote jugular venous outflow.
Which medications will be prescribed?	Anticonvulsants, antihypertensives, corticosteroids, diuretics
Teach the client not to ___, ___, or ____.	Strain, cough, or sneeze as these actions can increase ICP.
What are the nursing interventions?	Decrease environmental stimuli. Maintain body temperature. Limit fluid intake. Monitor intake and output.

Inflammatory Bowel Disease
Two primary types

	Crohn's Disease	Ulcerative Colitis
Location of Disease	Anywhere in the digestive tract from the mouth to anus	Primarily in the colon
Signs	3-4 semi-soft stools, diarrhea. No blood will be present. Anorexia, Fistulas Cobblestone appearance	Bloody diarrhea Lower abdominal cramps Weight loss Anemia may be present due to bleeding.
Lifestyle	Associated with smoking. High risk for malnutrition, malabsorption	Associated with non-smokers
Treatment	Anti-inflammatory amino salicylates Glucocorticoids NPO Status with bowel rest during flares Small frequent meals avoiding dairy and greasy foods. Low fiber will help relieve diarrhea. Surgery will not help; disease will continue to come back in other areas of the digestive system.	Anti-inflammatory steroids NPO Status with bowel rest during flare ups. Clients should limit intake of caffeine. Sigmoidoscopy is key for diagnosis. This condition is managed surgically to remove the affected area.

Influenza

What are the symptoms?	Cough, sore throat, fever, myalgias.
What isolation precautions are required?	Droplet.
What are the intervention methods to stop the spread?	Vaccination, early detection, personal quarantine, handwashing.
What pharmacological therapy can be given?	Antiviral agents to be given within 12 to 24 hours of symptoms. Example: oseltamivir.
What is the earliest age to get an influenza vaccine?	6 months of age.
What are the nursing interventions?	Monitor vital signs. Assess lung sounds. Administer analgesics, antipyretics, decongestants. Maintain droplet precautions.

Instillation of Ear Medications

The medication should be _____ temperature?	Room – too hot or cold will have side effects (nausea, dizziness etc.)
Which position should the client be placed in when receiving ear medication?	Supine, with affected ear up
When administering ear meds to an adult, draw the pinna back and _____.	Up
When administering ear meds to a child, draw the pinna back and _____.	Down
How many minutes should the head be tilted to allow medication to travel through the ear canal?	5 minutes.

Instillation of Eye Medications

When giving eye medications, do this to prevent medication from going into the lacrimal duct.	Apply pressure to the inner canthus.
Pull the _____ eye lid down against the _____.	lower, cheek.
Squeeze the drop in the _____ _____.	Conjunctival sac.
If more than one drop is prescribed, wait ___ to ___ minutes before applying another drop.	3 to 5 minutes
Do not let the _____ _____ touch the _____.	Medication bottle, eyeball

Integumentary System

What is the largest organ in the integumentary system?	The skin
What are the three types of glands in the integumentary system?	Sebaceous, sudoriferous, & ceruminous.
What is a gland?	Organ that secretes a chemical substance

What are the three layers of skin?	Epidermis (outer layer) Dermis (middle layer) Subcutaneous or Hypodermis (inner layer)
What is another name for eccrine gland?	Sweat gland
What is the function of the eccrine gland?	Secrete water through skin. This is an important function to cool the body.
What is the small opening of the skin where oil and sweat reach the surface?	Pore
What is the apocrine gland?	Sweat glands associated with hair glands.
What is the difference between eccrine glands and apocrine glands?	Eccrine glands go directly through the skin. Apocrine glands empty to a hair follicle.
Which vitamin does the skin absorb?	Vitamin D
Which layer of skin has the primary function of protection?	Epidermis
Which layer of skin connects to muscles and bones?	Hypodermis
Which layer of skin holds blood cells, sweat glands, and hair follicles?	Dermis
What is homeostasis?	A stable, constant internal environment.
What are some electrolytes excreted through the skin?	Sodium, chloride, magnesium
Which gland excretes minerals and electrolytes?	Sudoriferous gland
Which type of nerves allow the skin to feel pain, pressure, and temperature?	Sensory nerves
What is thermoregulation?	Process by which body maintains its internal core temperature?
How do blood vessels respond when the body is too warm?	They dilate (open)
How do blood vessels respond when the body is too cool?	They constrict (close)

Intravenous Therapy (IV)

Why are IV fluids used?	They are a quick way to replace nutrients, water, and electrolytes.
What are the three types of IV fluid?	Isotonic, hypotonic, and hypertonic.
What are isotonic fluids?	Isotonic fluids have a similar concentration to blood. This is important because the fluids will not cause water to move in or out of the cell. The size of the cell remains normal. Examples are: 0.9% normal saline, Lactated ringer, 5% dextrose in water (D5W)

| Why would the nurse give isotonic fluids? | In conditions such as diabetic ketoacidosis, or burns- to replace sodium and chloride and 0.9 % normal saline is always hung with blood** |

Why would the nurse give isotonic fluids?

In conditions such as diabetic ketoacidosis, or burns- to replace sodium and chloride and 0.9 % normal saline is always hung with blood**

What are hypotonic fluids?

A hypotonic fluid is less concentrated than the blood. This would cause water to move into the cell. The size of the cell increases. Examples are: 0.45% normal saline, 0.33% normal saline, 2.5% Dextrose water.

Hypotonic fluids should not be given for which conditions?

Clients with increased intracranial pressure, trauma, and skin burns. Hypotonic fluids will cause the cells to swell and create further damage. Also, hypotension as it lowers the blood volume.

Why would the nurse give hypotonic fluids?

In conditions such as dehydration, hypernatremia; and if the client needed their blood pressure to be lowered.

Why should hypotonic fluids be closely monitored?

A rapid increase of fluid shifting into the cells can cause cellular and cerebral edema.

What are hypertonic fluids?

Hypertonic fluids are more concentrated than the blood. This would cause water movement out of the cell. The size of the cell shrinks. Examples are: 5% normal saline, 5% dextrose in normal saline, 5% dextrose in lactated Ringer's, 5% dextrose in 0.45% normal saline.

Why would the nurse give hypertonic fluids?

In a condition such as hypovolemia (low blood pressure), hypertonic solutions can be given to increase blood pressure. Hypertonic solutions can provide sodium and other electrolytes while adding minimal water.

Why should hypertonic fluids be closely monitored?

It can cause electrolyte imbalance and dehydration.

Which conditions are contraindicated for hypertonic fluids?

Cellular dehydration, kidney damage and heart disease.

Before the nurse starts IV fluids the _____ _____ should be assessed.

Intravenous (IV) site.

Intravenous (IV) Complications

	Extravasation	Infiltration	Phlebitis
Definition	The leakage of a vesicant into intravascular tissue.	The leakage of an IV fluid or medication into extravascular tissue. *This medication/fluid is a non-vesicant.*	Inflammation of the vein
Cause	Dislodged catheter Occluded vein	Dislodged catheter Occluded vein	Irritating solutions Rapid infusion rates Prolonged use of the same catheter
Clinical Signs	Pain, redness, swelling, increased skin temperature at the site. Fluid leaking from the IV site.	Pain, redness, swelling, increased skin temperature at the site.	Pain, redness, swelling, increased skin temperature at the site.
Nursing Interventions	Stop IV infusion. Elevate the extremity. Prepare antidote if one is available. Monitor and photograph the site. Frequently monitor the site. *Do not remove the IV if it is a vesicant. Leave the catheter in place!	Stop the infusion. Elevate the extremity. Apply a warm compress. Insert a new IV catheter in the opposite extremity.	Stop the infusion. Frequently monitor the site. Apply a warm compress. Insert a new IV access in the opposite extremity.

Laminectomy

Surgery is the removal of _____ so the spinal cord can be seen.	Bone
To move the client after surgery, ____ ___ this client!	Log roll
What position must the client remain in?	Flat
The client is at risk for which type of infection?	Arachnoiditis

Laryngitis

What is laryngitis?	The inflammation of the voice box (larynx) from overuse, irritation, or infection.
What are the common symptoms of laryngitis?	Hoarseness, difficulty speaking, sore throat, mild fever, cough.
What are the most common causes?	A viral infection such as a cold or flu.
What should the client avoid?	Talking loudly, smoking, spending time in dusty environments, drinking too much caffeine or alcohol.
Acute laryngitis will be resolved in how many weeks?	2 weeks.
What is a complete loss of voice called?	Aphonia.
What is the common finding in acute and chronic laryngitis?	Reinke's edema
What is the most important intervention?	Voice rest is the single most important factor. Use of voice results in incomplete or delayed recovery. Complete voice rest is difficult to achieve.
When should the client seek medical emergency?	If they begin to have trouble breathing or cough up blood.

Lead Poisoning

What is the highest risk factor of ingesting lead?	Age: younger kids put things in their mouth.
What item is most likely to cause lead poisoning?	Lead paint chips.
The most dangerous side effect of children ingesting lead is _____ _____.	intellectual disability
What are the clinical signs of lead poisoning?	Headache, abdominal pain, fatigue muscle, weakness and respiratory depression. Increased clinical signs are based on dose.
How is lead poisoning treated?	Chelating agents.
How are the chelating agents given?	By administering many IM injections.
Do not give _____ _____ to induce vomiting.	Ipecac syrup.

 Study more at ReMarNurse.com | Join live weekly on YouTube @ReMarNurse

Legal Issues

Negligence is when a nurse does _____.

Not provide appropriate care according to set standards.

If a nurse does a treatment without consent, it is example of _____?

Battery.

If the client falls out of bed because the nurse forgot to put up the side rails, this is considered?

Neglect.

Any nursing action that has the word "threat" should be considered an _____.

Assault.

Advanced directives are important because they____.

Allow the client to direct how and what care they want to receive if they become unable to make decisions in the future.

Are advanced directives mandatory for a client?

No-they are optional.

The document that specifically names a person to make decisions on another person's behalf is a _____.

Durable power of attorney

The client must be of ____ ____ to write a will.

Sound mind.

Leukemia

Is leukemia a type of cancer?

Yes, leukemia is a type of cancer that affects the blood and bone marrow and is brought on by the rapid growth of abnormal WBCs

How is leukemia developed?

Leukemia appears to develop when some blood cells' genetic material (DNA) changes (mutations).

Is leukemia contagious?

Leukemia is not infectious. A virus or other infectious agent does not cause leukemia.

What are the main types of leukemia?

There are four broad classifications of leukemia: Acute lymphocytic leukemia (ALL) – occurs frequently in children.
Acute myelogenous leukemia (AML) – can occur in children and adults.
Chronic lymphocytic leukemia (CLL) – people over 55 years old are more likely to be affected.
Chronic myelogenous leukemia (CML) – It primarily affects adults.

Does a rash develop with leukemia?

Leukemia may produce petechiae, a rash like formation of pinpoint red patches on the skin. Petechiae are brought on by bleeding into the skin and decreased platelet counts.

How does leukemia affect blood function?

These abnormal white blood cells cannot fight infection and can affect the bone marrow's ability to produce RBC and platelets.

What safety measures should be taken for clients with leukemia?

Clients with leukemia, especially those on chemo are at higher risk of infection. Encourage infection control methods.

Does exposure to chemicals has a risk of leukemia?

Yes, long-term exposure to specific pesticides or industrial chemicals, such as benzene, is considered to increase the risk of leukemia.

How is leukemia treated?	Available treatment options for leukemia are chemotherapy, Chimeric Antigen receptor T-cell therapy (CAR) T-cell therapy, and targeted therapy.
Is there any medication that should be avoided for clients with leukemia?	Avoid using aspirin. Aspirin might cause gastrointestinal bleeding and lower platelet count.

Lung Cancer

What are the diagnostic exams involved?	Chest x-ray, CT scan, MRI which will show a lesion or mass.
What are some common causes of lung cancer?	Cigarette smoke or tobacco exposure, environmental pollutants
Is wheezing present?	Wheezing and hoarseness of voice is present
What is the best position for this client?	Fowler's position to help ease breathing.
Will this client gain weight or lose weight?	Anorexia and weight loss are observed.
Which diet is appropriate for clients with lung cancer?	High calorie, high-protein, high vitamin diet.
What is the contraindication during the MRI procedure?	An implanted pacemaker. This will interfere with the magnetic fields of the MRI scanner and may be deactivated by them.
True or false? Lung cancer is the highest killer among of cancer types.	True.
What is the nursing priority for these clients?	Airway is the top priority.
What is the most prevalent carcinoma of the lung?	Adenocarcinoma.

Lung Sounds

What is the cause of crackles?	Fluid or secretions in the airway.
When would the nurse hear crackles?	On inspiration
What are some possible causes of crackles?	Pneumonia, edema, or bronchitis.
What is another name for crackles?	Rales.
What are the characteristics of wheezes?	High-pitched musical sounds.
When would the nurse hear wheezes?	On inspiration and expiration.
What are the possible causes of wheezing?	Asthma, smoking, allergic reactions.
Wheezes can often be heard without a _____.	Stethoscope.
_____ air will help relieve symptoms of wheezing.	Humidified.
What is the characteristic of stridor?	A high-pitched harsh sound heard in the UPPER airway.
What are the causes of stridor?	Laryngeal spasm, swelling, croup and epiglottitis.

Stridor is often confused with _____.

Wheezing.

In which age group is stridor often seen?

Children.

Lyme Disease

This type of infection is caused by?

A bite from a tick

What are the clinical symptoms?

Fever, chills, and the bull's eye rash.

How long after a bite should a test be done?

Between 4 to 6 weeks

What is the treatment plan?

Take antibiotics:
Doxycycline (Adults)
Amoxicilin (Children)

Maslow's Hierarchy of Needs

What are the most important factors in order?

Physiological Needs
Safety and Security
Love and Belonging
Self-Esteem
Self-Actualization

Mastectomy

This surgery is to remove _____ or the _____.

Breast tissue or nipple.

After surgery, _____ the affected
arm to prevent _____.

Elevate, lymphedema.

No _____ _____or _____ in the affected arm.

Blood pressures, venipunctures.

Always assess the site for signs of
_____ after surgery.

Infection.

List signs of clinical site infection.

Swelling, redness, fever, chills,
elevated WBC count.

Medical Abbreviation

What is the medical abbreviation for ointment?

"Ung" unguentum.

What are differences between PC and AC?

PC – after meals
AC – before meals

Medication abbreviations are used?

BID – twice a day
TID – thrice a day
QID – four times a day
HS – bedtime

What does STAT means?

Immediately.

What is ABG?

Arterial Blood Gas.

What is the difference between a cubic centimeter
(cc) and milliliter (mL)?

They are the same measurement; there is
no difference in volume The primary.
difference is that milliliters are used for
fluid amounts while cubic centimeters are
used for solids.

What is PRN?

"as desired or as needed".

Abbreviation for right eye and left eye?	OD – oculus dexter "Right Eye" OS - oculus sinister "Left Eye"
Abbreviation for right ear and left ear?	AD – right ear AS – left ear AU – both ears
What is the abbreviation for pregnant?	G (Gravida)
What are the "Do Not Use" abbreviations?	

Do Not Use	Use Instead
U	Unit
OD, QD, qd, QOD,	Daily, every other day
Trailing zero Example (X.0 mg)	Write X mg or 0.X mg
< or >	Write greater than or less than

Medication Administration

What are the six rights of medication administration?	1. Patient 2. Medication 3. Documentation 4. Dose 5. Time 6. Route
What two verifiers can a client give before the nurse administers the medication?	Name and birthdate
Do not store medications ___ ___ ___.	At the bedside.
Can the nurse give medication prepared by another RN?	No, never do this! It is illegal.
What does it mean if a medication is PRN?	It means to give only when needed
Do not _____ sustained-release capsules or enteric-coated tablets.	Crush
What should a nurse do if she/he administers the wrong medication?	Notify physician; DO NOT document in client's chart but complete an incident form. This is not part of client records.

Meniere's Syndrome

What is it?	Meniere's syndrome is an inner ear disorder.
What are the symptoms?	Tinnitus, unilateral hearing loss, and dizziness.
What are the causes?	Viral and bacterial infections and allergic reactions.
Describe a Meniere's attacks.	It results in severe, sudden attacks that may cause permanent hearing loss. Nausea and vomiting can also be present.
What is the best environment for a client with this disease?	Bed rest in a quiet room, sedatives can be given to keep client calm. Low-playing music helps with the tinnitus. The client should move the head and ambulate slowly.

What should the client's diet be?	Low sodium to help reduce fluid overload in the ear.
Is surgery needed?	In severe cases a removal of the labyrinth (or labyrinthectomy) is performed.

Meningitis

What is meningitis?	Inflammation of arachnoid and pia mater of the brain and spinal cord.
How is it transmitted?	Direct contact and droplet.
What are the clinical signs?	Nuchal rigidity, tachycardia, headache, nausea, and vomiting.
Meningitis can also cause _____ _____ _____.	Increased intracranial pressure
What two physical signs are positive?	Positive Kernig's and Brudzinski sign.
What are the nursing interventions?	Monitor LOC, vital signs, initiate seizure precautions, maintain droplet isolation, and elevate the head of the bed.
What medications are prescribed?	Antibiotics and analgesics.

Menopause

What hormones are stopped during menopause?	Estrogen and progesterone.
True or False: Nicotine can cause early menopause.	True. Cigarette smoking may have an influence on ovarian aging and follicle reserve through altering gonadotropins and sex hormones, as well as having harmful effects on ovarian germ cells.
What are the signs that a client is already in her menopause?	Menopause age: 40-50 years old Mammary glands (breast) tenderness Menses changes Mood swings Menstrual migraines Musculoskeletal changes (osteoporosis) Mental changes Vasomotor symptoms (hot flashes) Vagina mucosae changes Vaginal atrophy (GSM: genitourinary syndrome of menopause)
What is the test to confirm menopause?	Hormone panel: Follicle-stimulating hormone and luteinizing hormone test.
Is perimenopause the same as premenopause?	No, premenopause happens around menopause and the client does not have menopausal symptoms. Perimenopause happens just before menopause and the client will start to experience some menopausal symptoms.
True or False: Hormone therapy can stop menopause.	No, hormone therapy's primary goal is to treat severe hot flashes and other menopausal symptoms.

Study more at ReMarNurse.com | Join live weekly on YouTube @ReMarNurse

What are the known contraindications of menopausal hormone therapy?	History of breast cancer, endometrial cancer, heart disease, thrombosis, embolism, liver disease, unexplained vaginal bleeding, transient ischemic attack.
The common complication of menopause is _____.	Osteoporosis.

Migraine

Are migraines and headaches the same?	No, headaches produce head, face, or upper neck pain and can vary in frequency and intensity. Migraines are characterized By more severe and incapacitating symptoms than headaches.
Does all migraines have a headache?	No, silent migraines also called a migraine aura without headache. It causes flashing lights but without pain in the head.
Can migraine be inherited?	Yes, migraine is greatly affected by genetics. This means that it is frequently passed down through families .
What are the phases of migraine?	**Prodrome:** The first stage and an early warning sign of a migraine. **Aura:** The aura phase may last 5 - 60 mins Some people experience both the aura and the headache at the exact moment. **Headache:** The headache can persist anywhere from 4 to 72 hrs. The sensation is described as drilling & throbbing in the head. **Postdrome:** This stage lasts for a day or two There are flashing lights, but no headache.
Does the menstrual cycle cause migraines?	Yes, estrogen fluctuations, such as before or during menstruations, pregnancy, and menopause stimulate migraine in many women.
Does sleeping relieve migraine?	Many clients report that sleeping helps to alleviate their migraine attacks. However, do not oversleep. An hour or two hours of sleep can be effective.
How should pain medication be taken?	Migraine pain medications work best when taken as prescribed and as soon as migraine symptoms appear.
How to keep a migraine journal?	Note of the following: Date and time the migraine started. Duration of pain. Pain scale. Pain location. Specific symptoms. Last food and drink consumed. Type of weather. Hours of sleep. Medication and treatment used. Other factors.

Study more at ReMarNurse.com | Join live weekly on YouTube @ReMarNurse

Military Time Chart

Standard time	Military time
12:00 am	0000
1:00 am	0100
2:00 am	0200
3:00 am	0300
4:00 am	0400
5:00 am	0500
6:00 am	0600
7:00 am	0700
8:00 am	0800
9:00 am	0900
10:00 am	1000
11:00 am	1100
12:00 pm	1200
1:00 pm	1300
2:00 pm	1400
3:00 pm	1500
4:00 pm	1600
5:00 pm	1700
6:00 pm	1800
7:00 pm	1900
8:00 pm	2000
9:00 pm	2100
10:00 pm	2200
11:00 pm	2300

Mongolian Spots

What do these spots look like?

Bluish-black spots on body.

Where are the spots found?

On the back and buttocks of newborns.

In which race are these spots mostly seen?

Asian and African Americans.

Are they harmful and how long do they appear?

No. They are normal in newborns and they gradually fade over time. They are not cancerous.

Movement Disorders: Chorea Seizures/Epilepsy

What is chorea?

Chorea = "dance"
- a movement disorder that causes involuntary muscle movements.

Who is affected by chorea?

- History of Huntington's disease.
- Children with rheumatic fever.
- Autoimmune diseases.
- Hormonal disorders.

What are the symptoms of chorea?

- Involuntary muscle movements.
- Milkmaid's grip.
- Harlequin tongue.
- Speech problems.
- Headaches and seizures.

How is chorea diagnosed?

Blood tests, MRI scan, CT scan, genetic testing.

What is epilepsy?

A brain disorder that causes recurring, unprovoked seizures.

What are the 2 types of seizure?	Generalized and partial. Partial seizures are also called focal seizures
What are the phases of seizure activity?	1. Prodromal 2. Aural 3. Ictal 4. Postictal
What are the clinical manifestations for epilepsy?	Aura, postictal state, todd paralysis, visual hallucinations, and convulsions.
What are the diagnostic tests for epilepsy?	CT scan, EEG, MRI and lumbar puncture.
When taking phenobarbital what needs to be avoided?	Avoid using sleep aids.

Multiple Sclerosis (MS)

True or false? MS is a chronic, progressive degenerative disease of the nervous system.	True
What part of the nervous system is affected?	The problem is with demyelination of the white matter of the brain and spinal cord.
Is there a cure for MS?	No.
What are the signs of MS?	Muscle spasms, weakness, bowel & bladder dysfunction numbness in the extremities, and visual disturbances.
Which medication will be given for spasms?	Baclofen
What medication will be given to reduce the amount of time a client experiences exacerbated symptoms?	Corticosteroids

Munchausen Syndrome

What is the definition of this syndrome?	A psychiatric disorder that causes a person to self-inflict injury to his/her own body. The person may also say that he/she has a mental disorder. This is all done to get attention from healthcare workers.
What is Munchausen syndrome by proxy (MSBP)?	An individual, typically a mother, intentionally causes or makes up an illness in a child under their care for attention.
What are the clinical observations?	The child will have issues with no explained etiology. Treatment of the issue does not stop the child from needing hospital visits. Assessments indicates the child is healthy, symptoms get better when child is away from the caregiver. Nursing priority: Protect the child!

Myasthenia Gravis

True or False? Myasthenia gravis is an autoimmune disease that results in extreme fatigue and muscle weakness.

True

What is the malfunction in the body?

The body produces antibodies that block acetylcholine receptors.

Is there a cure for myasthenia gravis?

No.

What are the clinical signs?

Difficulty talking, chewing, weak eye muscle visual disturbances, and unsteady gait.

Will the symptoms of myasthenia gravis worsen with activity?

Yes, they will.

The _____ test is performed to diagnose myasthenia gravis.

Tensilon

If the client's muscle strength is increased, the test is _____ for myasthenia gravis.

Positive.

What medication will be given?

Anticholinesterase-plasmapheresis is a possible treatment too.

Myocardial Infarction (MI)

What is the cause of an MI?

A decreased oxygen supply to heart.

Where is the pain felt?

Substernal (sudden, crushing, radiating to jaw, shoulders, back) & lasting longer than 30 minutes.

MI pain is not relieved by _____ or _____.

Rest or nitroglycerin.

What changes would you see on an EKG?

ST elevation inverted T waves.

What lab values will be elevated?

CK-MB
CPK
Troponin
LDH
WBC

Which medications are given for an MI?

M.O.N.A.
Morphine
O2
Nitroglycerin
Aspirin

In which order should MONA be administered?

Oxygen, nitroglycerin, aspirin, morphine O.N.A.M.

What activity is prescribed for this client?

Bed rest.

What is angina pectoris?

Chest pain due to the heart not receiving enough oxygen.

Where is the pain located?

The same area of the chest as reported in an MI.

What are some common causes of angina?

Early-morning activity, eating large meals, general stress, exercise, and smoking.

How is stable angina different from an MI?

Angina is chest pain that has a typical onset location, lasts for three to five minutes and is relieved by nitroglycerin or rest.

What is unstable angina?	It is chest pain that occurs while the client is resting.
Which diagnostic tests are utilized?	A cardiac catheterization. A coronary artery bypass, An exercise stress test. EKG, no ST elevation indicates angina instead of a MI.

Neomycin Sulfate

What is neomycin sulfate?	It's an aminoglycoside that reduces the number of bacteria in the colon.
Why does this matter?	It is given for the GI tract before surgery.
How is it used in clients with hepatic encephalopathy?	It can be used when ammonia levels are elevated in the liver.

Neuroleptic Malignant Syndrome (NMS)

When does this syndrome occur?	It could occur any time a client is on anti-psychotic medication, it is most common when the treatment begins or if doses are increased.
What are the signs of N.M.S.?	Tachycardia, extreme fever, altered LOC, seizures, muscle rigidity elevated, lab values (e.g., WBC and LFT)
What is the treatment?	Discontinue the medication. Initiate safety and seizure precautions. Give antipyretics to reduce fever.

Neuromuscular System

What two types of movements are controlled?	Voluntary and involuntary
What is another name for nerve cell?	Neuron
Where do nerves transmit signals from?	Central nervous system
What do nerve impulses travel along?	Axons
What wraps around and protects nerve fibers?	Myelin sheath
What are the neurons that carry signs to the central nervous system?	Sensory or afferent neurons
What are the neurons that carry signs from to the muscles?	Motor or efferent neurons brain/spinal cord out
Is singing a voluntary or involuntary action?	Voluntary
Is sneezing a voluntary or involuntary action?	Involuntary
What is the process when muscles become shorter and tighter?	Contraction
What is the nerve fiber that carries electrical impulses from the neuron?	Axon
What is the part of the peripheral nervous system that regulates involuntary functions?	Autonomic nervous system

What is the unconscious action performed as a response to a stimuli?	Reflex
What is the process of a muscle releasing tension and pressure?	Relaxation
What is the structure that allows one neuron to communicate with another neuron?	Synapse
What is a stretch or tear in a muscle ligament?	A sprain
What is a stretch or tear in a muscle tendon?	A strain
Is a sprain and a strain the same thing?	No, the location is different.
What is muscular dystrophy?	A genetic disorder of progressive weakening of skeletal muscles.

Nasogastric (NG) Tube

What position should the client be in during the NG tube placement?	High Fowler's with hand tilted forward.
The NG tube goes from the ____ to ____.	Nose to stomach.
What is a Salem sump?	Double lumen of NG tube used to decompress the stomach.
What are the measuring points for determining the length of insertion?	Nose to earlobe to xiphoid process.
If the client starts to gag during placement should the nurse continue the procedure?	Yes, wait for client to stop gagging or coughing, then continue to advance; offer water to help the tube go down.
What should be done before using the NG tube for the first time?	X-ray, aspirate for gastric content (pH should be less than 4).
If the NG tube is to suction, should the nurse turn off the suction when medications are given orally?	Yes, for at least 30 minutes.
If a client vomits during the procedure should the nurse keep going with the NG tube?	Yes, wait for few minutes, then proceed. Let the client know that they will feel better once the NG tube is in place.

Nitroglycerin

What is the action of nitroglycerin?	Systemic and coronary vasodilation.
What conditions are treated by nitroglycerin?	Angina, cocaine abuse, it can be given before activities that cause chest pain.
If nitroglycerin is given sublingually for angina pain and it is not relieved, what should the nurse do?	Give an additional tablet in five minutes. Up to three tablets can be taken over 15 minutes. The client should call 911 after the first dose.

 Study more at ReMarNurse.com | Join live weekly on YouTube @ReMarNurse

If nitroglycerin is given SL and the client reports as stinging sensation, is that normal?	Yes, it means the tablet is fresh.
What is the most common side effect reported?	Headache.
What are other common side effects?	Hypotension, tachycardia, dizziness, and syncope.
If a client has on a transdermal ointment or nitroglycerin patch, should the nurse rotate sites during application?	Yes, to prevent skin irritation.
Do not place a nitroglycerin patch over a _____.	Pacemaker.
The client's nitroglycerin patch should be removed before having a _____ scan.	MRI.
Should a client take nitroglycerin prophylactically before sex?	Yes, to prevent chest pain
If a male client is taking sildenafil, what should the nurse tell him?	Don't take with nitroglycerin.
IV nitroglycerin and all IV dysrhythmics should be placed on an _____ _____.	Infusion pump
What is verapamil used for?	Used to treat blood pressure and angina.

NSAIDs

What does it stand for?	Nonsteroidal Anti-Inflammatory Drugs.
What type of drugs are they?	Aspirin and aspirin-like drugs.
What do NSAIDs do?	Reduce pain and body temperature and and inhibit platelet and inhibit platelet aggregation.
Clients should take NSAIDs with a full glass of _____ or _____ to prevent stomach irritation.	Water, milk
Aspirin toxicity will cause _____ in the ears.	Tinnitus.
Teach clients to avoid _____ when taking NSAIDs to decrease stomach irritation.	Alcohol
NSAIDs increase/decrease bleeding potential.	Increase
How soon should a client stop taking NSAIDs before having surgery?	1 week.
Children shouldn't take NSAIDs when they have flu-like symptoms due to the risk of?	Reye's syndrome.

Obsessive Compulsive Disorder (OCD)

What is the defining characteristic of OCD?

OCD is characterized by a pattern of unwanted ideas and fears (obsessions) that leads to a repetitive behavior (compulsions).

Are OCD and OCPD the same thing?

OCPD is a personality condition characterized by an obsession with perfectionism, organization, and control.

People with OCD usually know that their obsessions and compulsions are unpleasant and recognize that they require professional help to cure the disorder.

People with OCPD frequently believe nothing is wrong with their actions or views.

What are the 4 general categories of OCD?

Checking, contamination, symmetry and ordering, ruminations, and intrusive thoughts.

Is OCD inherited?

Yes, according to research, those with a parent or sibling with OCD are more likely to develop this disorder.

Is there any prevention for OCD?

OCD cannot be prevented. However, early detection and treatment could lessen symptoms and their effect in life.

What infection in children is commonly related to OCD?

In some cases, children may develop OCD following a streptococcal infection. This is called pediatric autoimmune neuropsychiatric disorders associated with streptococcal infections, PANDAS.

Can OCD be treated?

There is no treatment for OCD. However, symptoms that interfere with daily life can be managed with medication, therapy, or a combination of treatments.

Obstetrics History

What is GTPAL?

An acronym to remember essential information in an obstetric history.

What do the letters stand for?

Gravidity, term, preterm, abortion, & living.

What does the gravidity number mean?

It is the number of times a woman has been pregnant, including the current pregnancy.

What does the term number mean?

It is how many full-term births a client has had. This is an infant born after 37-weeks.

What does the preterm number mean?

It is the number of births where the age of the infant is from greater than 20 to 36.6 weeks.

What does the abortion number mean?

It is a general term meaning a pregnancy that has ended without a live birth. An abortion can be induced or spontaneous.

What does the living number mean?

This number represents how many living children the client currently has.

Orthostatic Hypotension

What is it?

Systolic or diastolic BP drops more than 10 mm Hg and heart rate increases by 10-20 when the client changes position (lying, sitting, and standing) The blood pressure will go down and the heart rate will go up.

How will client feel?

Dizzy, light-headed, unsteady.

How to assess for orthostatic hypotension?

The nurse should check the blood pressure while client is lying down, sitting up, and standing. Wait five minutes between measurements.

What is the treatment?

IV fluids for volume replacement.

What are the safety concerns?

This client is a fall risk.

Osteoarthritis

What is osteoarthritis?

A degenerative disease of the joints.

Osteoarthritis is the _____ _____ form of arthritis seen in the elderly.

Number one.

Which joints in the body are most affected?

Weight-bearing joints -knees, hips, fingers, back.

What are the clinical signs of osteoarthritis?

Limited joint mobility, joint pain, joint stiffness.

Is the pain from osteoarthritis relieved by activity or rest?

Rest.

Hard nodes will develop on the joints of the fingers, creating deformities. What is this called?

Heberden's nodes or Bouchard nodes

What is the primary medication given for pain?

NSAIDs

_____ may be injected into the joints to treat osteoarthritis.

Corticosteroids.

What should the nurse teach the client concerning activity?

Stop exercise if pain occurs. Try to lose weight to help take stress off joints. Use hot or cold therapy to help with pain. Assistive devices (canes, braces, etc.) will help with mobility.

What surgery may be required?

Hip and knee replacements.

Osteoporosis

How does osteoporosis affect bone?

Osteoporosis weakens the bones, causing them to be more prone to fractures which can happen suddenly and unexpectedly.

What causes osteoporosis?

Osteoporosis is caused by a rapid loss of bone mass than the normal.

What hormonal imbalance may cause osteoporosis?

Estrogen deficiency, excess thyroid hormone.

What tests determines the mineral proportion in the bones?

Bone mineral density (BMD) test or dual-energy, X-ray absorptiometry (DEXA or DXA) scans.

What vitamins improve bone health?	Vitamin D.
Which drugs might hinder the bone-rebuilding process?	Long-term usage of corticosteroid drugs, such as prednisone and cortisone, either orally or intravenously, disrupts the bone- rebuilding process.
Does osteoporosis only affect older people?	No, it often occurs later in life, particularly in women following menopause. However, children and teenagers can acquire juvenile osteoporosis. This most commonly occurs in children aged 8 to 14.
What condition is called a "hunchback" or "round back" that results from osteoporosis?	Kyphosis.
What is the treatment for osteoporosis?	Exercise, vitamin, mineral supplements and medications may be used to treat diagnosed osteoporosis.
Can osteoporosis be prevented?	Yes, diet and lifestyle are two significant factors that you could change to help prevent osteoporosis.

Otitis Media

This is an infection of the _____ear.	Middle.
Why are children more prone to this?	Because their eustachian tubes are shorter than those of adults.
What are the signs?	Fever, loss of appetite, rolling head from side to side (This promotes ear drainage when it is done).
What is the treatment?	Analgesics and antibiotics.
What causes otitis media?	Bacteria and viruses cause ear infections. Frequently following a cold or other upper respiratory illness. The bacteria enters the middle ear and causes swelling of the eustachian tubes.
Is otitis media contagious?	Ear infections are not contagious, but the virus and/or bacteria that cause the infection are.
What are the different types of otitis media?	Acute otitis media, otitis media with effusion, chronic otitis media with effusion.
How common is otitis media?	Otitis media is the most common condition in children, except for colds. Ear infections mostly occur from ages 6 mo. to 8 yrs. old.
Does otitis media cause hearing loss?	Yes. During an ear infection, temporary hearing loss or changes in hearing (muffling or sound distortions) may be experienced. Repeated infections or damage to internal structures in the ear might result in more severe hearing loss.
Does otitis media result in complications?	The majority of ear infection do not have long-term complications.

Ovarian Cancer

What is ovarian cancer?

It is a cancer that forms in the tissues of the ovary.

What is the cause?

Obesity, endometriosis, family history or ovarian cancer. A woman who is not pregnant or having children.

What are the common sites of metastasis?

This occurs with a direct spread in the pelvis or lymphatic drainage.

This condition is most common in who?

Caucasian women ages 55 to 65 years of age. Also, of a North American and European descent.

What type of surgery is used to diagnose & stage ovarian cancer?

An exploratory laparotomy is performed to diagnose and stage the tumor.

Will the CA-125 tumor maker be high or low?

In assessing the client with ovarian cancer, the tumor marker (CA-125) is elevated.

What type of therapy may be used if the tumor has invaded to other organs?

1. External radiation therapy.
2. Chemotherapy is used post- operatively for most stages of ovarian cancer.
3. Intraperitoneal chemotherapy. Involves the instillation of chemotherapy into the abdominal cavity.

What is TAHBSO?

It is a total abdominal hysterectomy and bilateral salpingo-oophorectomy.

Clients are at risk for what other type of cancer?

Clients with ovarian cancer are at risk for breast cancer also.

A client with ovarian cancer should recognize what typical manifestation to be observed?

Abdominal distention

What cytotoxic agents are used to treat ovarian cancer?

Altretamine is a cytotoxic is used to treat ovarian cancer.

Oxygen Delivery Systems

What is the range of the flow rate for a nasal cannula?

The flow rate ranges from 1-6 LPM.

Why is the oxygen flow rate for a nasal cannula below 6?

Nares and mucosa dry out when the the rate is high.

What are the benefits of using a nasal cannula?

The client can still eat, drink, talk.

How often should the nasal cannula be changed?

Every day.

What should be inspected daily due to irritation?

Skin on face, nares, ears.

What is the flow rate range for a simple mask?

6-10 LPM.

When applying the mask, what must be done?

Make sure it fits properly, covering mouth and nose.

Clients wearing a face mask may feel _____.

Claustrophobic.

What makes a Venturi mask different from a regular face mask?

It allows the nurse to control how much room air is to be mixed with oxygen.

Always use a Venturi mask for clients with ____.	C.O.P.D. because the specific O2 concentration should be noted.
A partial rebreather mask looks like a face mask with a _____ _____ attached to it.	Reservoir bag.
Like the other forms of oxygen delivery, the partial rebreather allows ___ ___ to mix with ___ ____.	Room air, pure oxygen.
The reservoir bag should be inflated when?	At all times. Please note this.
The non-rebreather mask does not allow _____ _____	Room air to be inhaled.
How would you assess to see if the oxygen delivery system is effective?	A pulse oximetry reading, respiration rate and pattern, arterial blood gas.
Do not use ____ _____ for moisturizing the nares.	Petroleum jelly can set the client's face on fire. Use a water-soluble jelly.

Pacemakers

| What is the indication? | To conduct electrical activity and maintain a normal heart rate. |
| Describe client education on pacemakers. | Check pulse daily. Avoid large magnetic fields (MRI, industrial equipment). Household appliances are clear for use. Avoid contact sports. Report signs of dizziness, fatigue, or SOB to the doctor. Use cellphones on the opposite side of pacemaker. |

Pancreatitis (Acute)

What is the number-one cause of acute pancreatitis?	Alcohol abuse.
What are the symptoms of acute pancreatitis?	Abdominal pain, nausea, & vomiting, board-like abdomen. Skin discoloration (Cullen's and Turner's sign)
Will eating make the pain better or worse?	Worse, especially fatty foods.
Which liver enzymes are elevated with pancreatitis?	Lipase and amylase.
What are the nursing interventions?	Make the client NPO. An NG tube may be needed to reduce gastric distention, IV fluids to prevent dehydration. The client should be educated on the detrimental effects of alcohol.
How is the pain treated?	Demerol or hydromorphone.
Never give this for pain. Why?	Morphine; it was thought to cause spasms in pancreatic duct and sphincter of Oddi.

Paracentesis

| This is an invasive procedure. The client will need an ____ _____. | Informed consent. |
| This procedure collects fluid from where? | Peritoneal cavity of abdomen |

What to do before the procedure?	Measure abdomen, weigh the client and take the vital signs. Have the client void to empty bladder before the procedure.
What position should the client be in during this procedure?	Sitting on edge of the bed
What should the nurse do after the procedure?	Monitor the vital signs, measure the fluid collected, apply a sterile dressing to the insertion site and monitor for bleeding. Make sure urine is not bloody.

Parkinson's Disease

This disease is caused by a depletion of _____?	Dopamine
What are the signs of Parkinson's disease?	Bradykinesia, tremors in the hands and feet at rest, rigidity, shuffling steps, and loss of balance.
Is this disease process fast or slow?	Slow, progressive.
What are the nursing interventions?	Assess the neuro status and swallowing ability assist with ambulation, encourage fluids to prevent dehydration. Recommend high calorie & fiber meals with a low-protein diet.
Which medications are prescribed?	Anti-Parkinson's Anti-cholinergics.
When taking anti-cholinergics, clients should increase _____ to avoid _____.	Fiber, constipation
What are the other side effects of anti-cholinergics?	Blurred vision, dry mouth, photophobia, tachycardia. *Urinary retention & reduced tears
Which medications will be given to replace dopamine?	Levodopa or Carbidopa-levodopa.
Do not take dopamine replacement medications with _____ , as this may cause a hypertensive crisis.	MAOIs
Teach clients taking Parkinson's drugs to follow a ____ _____ diet.	Low-protein.
What vitamin should be avoided in the diet?	B6, which blocks the Parkinson's medication therapeutic effect.

Peptic Ulcer Disease

What bacteria is responsible for most peptic ulcers?	H. pylori
Where are most peptic ulcers found?	Gastric and duodenum
When a client has ulcers, what will the vomit look like?	"Coffee ground" emesis
When a client has ulcers, what will The stool look like?	"Black tarry"
What medications should be avoided?	NSAIDs
Is acetaminophen an NSAID?	No

Ulcers	Gastric	Duodenal
Where are the ulcers?	Stomach	Duodenum
Does stomach acid increase?	No, normal production	Yes, increased production
Where does the pain occur?	Mid-epigastric region	Mid-epigastric region
When does the pain occur?	With meals or after eating "starve a gastric ulcer"	On an empty stomach "feed a duodenal ulcer"

What type of medication will be given to decrease gastric acid production in duodenal ulcers?

H2 blockers and proton pump inhibitors.

What are medication examples of H2 blockers?

Ranitidine & Cimetidine

What are the medication examples of proton pump inhibitors?

Generic ending in "-zole"
Esomeprazole
Pantoprazole
Omeprazole

_____ are prescribed to neutralize gastric acid.

Antacids

What should the nurse teach clients with ulcers to avoid?

Smoking and alcohol
Spicy and greasy foods
Citrus fruits may irritate

Peripheral Arterial Disease (PAD)

PAD is an occlusive disease of the ___ ____.

lower extremities.

Will the damage to surrounding tissue occur above or below the arterial occlusion?

Below.

Would a pulse be felt in a leg with PAD?

No, it would be absent.

What would the leg look like?

Hairless, cool, pale, with thick toenails.

What is intermittent claudication?

Muscle pain from a decreased blood supply: the pain comes and goes.

The nurse should teach the client to avoid?

Smoke, wear tight clothing, or apply direct heat to the legs.

The nurse should teach the client to?

Exercise, inspect skin daily, take prescribed medications.

What procedures improve PAD?

Bypass surgery, angioplasty.

What does a leg with a venous occlusion look like?

Brown or purple discoloration, edema, or weeping fluid.

Pheochromocytoma

A tumor that produces an excessive amount of ____ and _____.

Epinephrine, norepinephrine.

This is a problem with the _____ gland.

Adrenal.

The clients will experience:

Sustained hypertension, sweating, weight loss, hyperglycemia and headache.

What is the treatment for pheochromocytoma:

Surgical removal of one or both adrenal glands.

What will the client need to take after surgery?

Glucocorticoid replacement.

Piaget's Theory of Cognitive Development

Age/Stage	Characteristics
Birth to 2 years - *Sensorimotor*	Child learns about reality by interacting with his/her environment.
2 to 7 years - *Preoperational*	Child moves on to pre-logical thinking; learns past, present, future. No abstract thinking yet.
7 to 11 years - *Concrete*	Child moves to logical thinking; able to classify and sort facts. Abstract thinking available. UNDERSTAND DEATH by 10 years old.
11 to adult - *Formal*	Person is able to think and learn as an adult; concrete and abstract reasoning is available.

Age/Stage	Clinical Priorities
Birth to 2 years - *Sensorimotor*	The child learns through the 5 senses, imitates behaviors, develops object permanence. The beginning of goal-directed actions.
2 to 7 years - *Preoperational*	The child has a one-way logic with the ability to use symbols, egocentrism, children has difficulty with the principle of conservation.
7 to 11 years - *Concrete*	The child uses hands on thinking, understands the need for an identity, and can understand classification.
11 to adult - *Formal*	Person is able to understand scientific reasoning, the nurse is able to explain difficult medical issues. Not all individual reach this stage depending on other medical or psychological factors.

Placenta Previa vs Abruptio Placenta

What is Abruptio Placenta?

When the placenta detaches itself from the uterine wall.

What is Placenta Previa?

The placenta is covering or near the cervix, blocking the opening to the vagina.

	Signs	Risk Factors	Dangers	Nursing Interventions
Abruptio Placenta	Sudden, PAINFUL, bleeding with contractions and uterine tenderness	HTN, diabetes, smoking, alcohol (ETOH) abuse, substance abuse	-Decreased oxygen and nutrients to fetus -Premature birth -Blood clots	Bed rest C-section if baby is term Frequent vitals Blood transfusion may be needed so a type and cross of the mother should be ordered.
Placenta Previa	Sudden, PAINLESS, bleeding, bright red in color Usually seen in third trimester	Previous C-section, multiparity, older-age mother	-Maternal hemorrhage -Premature labor	Bed rest C-section if baby is term Frequent vitals Blood transfusion may be needed so a type and cross of the mother should be ordered.

Both conditions will require which three interventions?

Frequent vitals fetal ultrasound Fetal heart monitoring.

Which condition has more bleeding?

Placenta previa

Which condition will create a rigid, board-like abdomen?

Abruptio placenta

Abruptio placenta causes which blood clotting disorder?

Disseminated intravascular coagulation (DIC)

If a pregnant client is bleeding vaginally the nurse should avoid a:

A vaginal exam

Plasmapheresis

What is plasmapheresis?

It is removing antibodies that attack the immune system from a client's plasma.

What kind of clients need plasmapheresis?

Clients with systemic lupus erythematosus, multiple sclerosis, Guillain-Barre and other autoimmune diseases.

	When plasma is removed what is it replaced by?	Saline or albumin
	During plasmapheresis is just the plasma removed?	No whole blood is removed then the plasma is separated.
	How long does a plasma exchange take?	1 to 3 hours.
	What is a potential complication of plasmapheresis?	Hypotension

When plasma is removed what is it replaced by?	Saline or albumin
During plasmapheresis is just the plasma removed?	No whole blood is removed then the plasma is separated.
How long does a plasma exchange take?	1 to 3 hours.
What is a potential complication of plasmapheresis?	Hypotension

Pleural Effusion

Pleural effusion is the collection of _____ in the pleural space.	Fluid.
What are the signs?	Sharp pain on inspiration tachycardia, decreased breath sounds and shortness of breath.
What is the treatment?	Find the cause, monitor breath sounds, performing a thoracentesis.
After a thoracentesis is performed, what may be needed temporarily?	A chest tube to remove residual fluid.
What medication can be prescribed if the fluid is not a large enough amount to perform a thoracentesis?	Diuretic.

Plegias

	Definition	Causes	Symptoms	Therapy
Paraplegia	Paralysis from the waist down, which can involve the inability to move the legs and affects the normal functioning of the lower body, such as bowel and bladder emptying and elimination	Spinal cord injury from a car accident, penetrating injuries (particularly from gunshot or stab wounds), and falls. Other common causes: Spine tumors, Spinal cord infection Ischemia Diabetes-related nerve damage Cerebral palsy Autoimmune or inflammatory conditions.	Loss of sensation in the lower part of the body. Unexplained pain in the lower body. Bowel and bladder difficulty. Walking and standing issues. Weight gain. Depression Sexual dysfunction Skin breakdown Infections High blood pressure	Surgery to manage swelling at the location of the injury. Medication to help lower the risk of infection, blood clots, and other side effects. Physical therapy assists in regaining as much function as possible by training. Occupational therapy. To help learn new abilities, restore old ones, and find new ways to function around injuries.
Hemiplegia	This paralysis affects only one side of the body. Facial paralysis conditions like Bell's palsy.	-Strokes or transient ischemic attacks (TIAs). -Aneurysms and hemorrhages in the brain.	Hemiplegia is the primary symptom of a stroke, which can be a life-threatening medical condition.	Some physical therapists may advise a wheelchair, walker, cane, or brace. Electrical stimulation seeks to promote brain plasticity and minimize imbalances in the damaged side of the brain.
Quadriplegia	Quadriplegia is paralysis that affects the entire body from the neck down. Tetraplegia is another name for this type of paralysis. This type of paralysis affects all limbs and body parts below the location of the injury.	The nerves that transmit information from the brain to muscles in the limbs are disrupted. Infection. Viruses and bacteria may damage nerve tissues. Birth defects, such as cerebral palsy and muscular dystrophy, which damage the muscles.	The primary sign of quadriplegia is weakness in all four limbs. Quadriplegia causes trouble regulating the muscles in the affected parts of the body. Flaccid quadriparesis: limp, unfirm muscles Muscle stiffness or tightness that is unusual (spastic quadriplegia) Loss of motor control Difficulty walking Urinary incontinence Lowered reflexes	Medication. Immunosuppressive medicines, for example, may be used to treat autoimmune or inflammatory disorders. Medication that corrects an electrolyte imbalance can be used to treat it. Other therapies may include: Surgery Muscle relaxants Pain relievers Physical therapy Occupational therapy Resistance exercise

Pneumonia

What is pneumonia?	An infection that inflames the air sacs (alveoli) in one or both lungs.
What is the possible ABG of a client with severe pneumonia?	Respiratory acidosis
What time of season does pneumonia usually occur?	The fall and winter
What is "walking" pneumonia?	It is a non-medical term for a mild case of pneumonia. The client can go about their daily activities. It is also known as mycoplasma pneumonia.
What is the most common bacteria causing pneumonia?	Streptococcus pneumoniae.
What sound would be heard by the nurse on auscultation?	Wheezing and crackles
What do you call a type of pneumonia that occurs when food, secretions, and liquids enter the lungs?	Aspiration pneumonia
How is pneumonia diagnosed?	Chest x-ray, sputum culture, and complete blood count.
What are the clinical signs of pneumonia?	Remember: PNEUMONIA **P**roductive cough & pain **N**eurological changes **E**levated labs PCO2 > 45 Increased WBC **U**nusual breath sounds, course crackles, wheezing **M**ild to high fever **O**xygen saturation decreases **N**ausea and vomiting **I**ncreased heart rate **A**ching all over
What are different types of pneumonia?	Ventilator assisted Community-acquired Aspiration Hospital Acquired Viral pneumonia Bacterial pneumonia

Polycythemia Vera

What is polycythemia vera?	A disorder of an increased number of erythrocytes, platelets, leukocytes, and the result is thickened blood.
What symptoms will be present?	Headache, SOB, & weakness, blurred vision inflammation
On assessment, what is seen?	Purple/red complexion, enlarged spleen, and increased hemoglobin.
With polycythemia, will clotting be increased or decreased?	Increased.
What is the main treatment?	Phlebotomy (blood draws several times a year)

 Study more at ReMarNurse.com | Join live weekly on YouTube @ReMarNurse

Post-Traumatic Stress Disorder (PTSD)

What causes PTSD?

Any traumatic event can cause PTSD.

What are the signs associated with PTSD?

Nightmare, anxiety attacks sleep disturbance, memory loss, or hypervigilance.

These clients will often seem detached. True or false?

True; clients will isolate themselves.

Clients with PTSD are at increased risk for ___ ___.

Substance abuse.

What is the treatment for PTSD?

Therapy to discuss feelings, Anxiety and depression meds, and support groups.

Preeclampsia

Preeclampsia usually occurs at which gestational age?

After 20 weeks of gestation

What are the major signs of preeclampsia?

Hypertension, edema, and proteinuria.

What is HELLP syndrome?

Hemolysis, Elevated liver enzymes and low platelets. This is a life-threatening condition

What is the position for mild preeclampsia?

Provide bed rest and place the client in the lateral position.

What are the criteria for a client to be diagnosed?

The criteria are based on three things:
1. blood pressure measurement
2. results of a urine sample (proteinuria)
3. signs of organ injury.

What is considered proteinuria for preeclampsia?

+ with a dipstick test 300 mg with a 24-hr urine 0.3 mg/dL creatinine/protein ratio.

What are some risk factors for preeclampsia?

History of preeclampsia, First pregnancy (primigravida), Obese (BMI> 30) Age (young less than 18, advanced over 35).

If the kidney is compromised will uric acid and creatinine be high or low?

Uric acid and creatinine levels will increase and urinary output will decrease.

Will the liver enzymes increase or decrease?

The liver is affected due to decreased tissue perfusion and swelling. The liver enzyme increase with AST and ALT are present.

What is the treatment for preeclampsia?

Remember! Do PREECLAMPSIA
Proteinuria monitoring
Reflexes hyperactive
Evaluate blood pressure
Edema monitoring
Calcium gluconate: antidote for magnesium sulfate toxicity
Left side lying position
Assess for seizure activity
Magnesium sulfate
Protein rich diet
Severe complications to watch for:
   Fetal distress or growth restriction
   HELLP syndrome stroke, placental abruption, DIC
Intake & Output: Monitoring
Antihypertensives

Pregnancy Stuff

Rho (D) immune globulin is given to pregnant clients who are Rh _____ but have a Rh_____ baby.

Negative, positive

When is Rho (D) immune globulin given?

At 28 weeks' gestation and within 72 hours after delivery It is given twice. This medication prevents the mom from developing antibodies against future Rh positive babies.

Is Rho (D) immune globulin given if the client has a miscarriage?
Is Rho (D) immune globulin given to the infant?

Yes, if the pregnancy is greater than 13 weeks.
No, never or to the father.

What are tocolytics?

Drugs given to stop preterm labor.

What is the mnemonic used to remember the four drugs that can be used for preterm labor?

It's Not My Time

Which medications do the letters stand for?

Indomethacin (NSAID)
Nifedipine (C.C.B.)
Magnesium sulfate
Terbutaline

When giving these medications, what must be monitored continuously?

Fetal heart rate and maternal vital signs.

Magnesium sulfate will decrease _____ _____, _____ _____ _____ and _____.

urine output, deep tendon, reflexes and respirations.

If a client is given terbutaline, watch for _____.

Tachycardia

Which two drugs are never given to a pregnant client? Think "Two QTs say no to OB's"

Quinolones, tetracyclines.

The umbilical cord in a newborn has _____ arteries and _____ vein.

2, 1
To easily remember, think AVA

Presbycusis

This is a form of _____ loss.

Hearing

Is presbycusis a natural process?

Yes

_____ voice tones are hardest to hear.

High

How should the nurse communicate with this client?

Facing towards the Client. The client should be encouraged to wear a hearing aid.

Pressure Ulcer

What are pressure ulcers?

Injury to skin and underlying tissue as a result of prolonged pressure to the skin.

How are pressure ulcers measured?

The Braden scale

What are the clinical symptoms of a stage 1 pressure ulcer?

Red, warm, intact skin that doesn't blanche.

What is an example of a stage 1 pressure ulcer?

It looks like a sunburn.

How would you describe a stage 2 pressure ulcer?	Superficial damage to the skin (epidermis or dermis). There will be a break in the skin.
What are some examples of a stage 2 pressure ulcer?	Abrasion, blisters, shallow craters.
What is a clinical sign of a stage 3 pressure ulcer?	Skin that is deeply damaged, but does not extend through fascia.
What is a clinical sign of a stage 3 pressure ulcer?	Deep crater.
What are clinical signs of a stage 4 pressure ulcer?	The skin is deeply damaged, the wound shows muscle tissues and ligaments.
What are some nursing interventions to prevent pressure ulcers from developing?	Turn client every two hours; keep the skin clean and dry; Encourage proper diet and hydration; Inspect skin and document daily.

Prostate Cancer

What are the risk factors for prostate cancer?	Advancing age heavy metal exposure, smoking, history of sexually transmitted infection.
Which race is most affected?	African Americans
Which type of nodule will be observed?	A hard pea-sized nodule or irregularities palpated on rectal examination.
What are the late symptoms of prostate cancer?	Weight loss, urinary obstruction, bone pain radiating from the lumbosacral area.
Will the prostate specific antigen level be high or low?	The prostate specific antigen level is elevated.
What is TURP?	Transurethral resection of the prostate (TURP) is a surgery used to treat urinary problems that are caused by an enlarged prostate.
What type of surgery is the removal of the prostate gland without opening the bladder?	Retropubic prostatectomy is the removal of prostate gland by a low abdominal incision without opening the bladder.
What should the nurse monitor postoperative TURP?	Severe hyponatremia (water intoxication) caused by the excessive absorption of bladder irrigation during surgery.

Radiation Therapy

What are the types of therapy?	External (outside body) -Beam and sealed Internal (inside body)
What are the side effects?	Alopecia, fatigue, and skin irritation.
Clients receiving beam radiation therapy should wash the area with?	Unscented soap and water then pat dry.
Clients receiving radiation therapy need private a _____ and _____.	Room, bathroom.

No ____ _____ or ____ _____ may come to visit.

Pregnant women or small kids.

Can a woman with a removed cervical implant have sexual intercourse?

Yes, 7-10 days after removal.

Nursing considerations:

Do not apply lotions, ointments, or powders to irradiated skin.

Raynaud's Disease

What is it?

Vasospasms of the arteries of the upper & lower extremities.

Which body parts are most affected?

Fingers, toes, and cheeks.

What does the client feel?

Numbness, tingling, and swelling; area may feel cold to the touch.

What are the treatments?

Monitor pulses, vasodilators, avoid cold and stress, stop smoking and wear warm clothes.

Respiratory System

Which gas is considered the waste during ventilation?

Carbon dioxide

A large tube that is reinforced by cartilage rings is called?

Trachea

What is a passage of airway that conducts air into the lungs?

Bronchus

What are the two bronchus called?

Bronchi

What are the small passages that connect bronchi to alveoli.

Bronchioles

What substance is produced to keep the lungs from collapsing?

Surfactant

Is the heart located on the left or right side of the chest?

Left

What is the name of the cavity that the lungs are in?

Pleural

Is diffusion a passive or active form of gas exchange?

Passive

The muscles in between the ribs are called?

Intercostal muscles

The amount of air breathed in and out of the lungs?

Tidal volume

Residual capacity is the amount of _____ trapped in the alveoli after expiration.

Air

As volume increases in the lungs the pressure _____.

Decreases

The passage of fluid to an organ is called _____.

Perfusion

These microscopic hair-like structures keep the lungs clear of mucous, bacteria, and dirt.

Cilia

What is the disease caused by an infection of fungus?	Mycosis
What is the highly contagious viral infection of the nose, throat, and lungs?	Influenza
Influenza is caused by several of the viruses found in which group?	Coronavirus
Influenza is always caused by a virus. True or false?	True, influenza is never caused by bacteria.
Which lung condition is due to damage to the alveoli?	Emphysema is the lung disease which causes shortness of breath.
What is the bacteria responsible for tuberculosis?	Mycobacterium
What are some of the signs of tuberculosis?	Low grade fever Night sweats Chest pain Weight loss
Is there a cure for tuberculosis?	Yes it is curable with drug combinations.
Which isolation is required for tuberculosis?	Airborne, this disease is very contagious.
_____ _____ liquid that allows the alveoli to open and prevents collapse.	Lung surfactant
What are the three types of blood cells?	Red blood cells (RBC), white blood cells (WBC), and platelets.
Which type of blood cell helps fight infection?	White
Which type of blood cell help carry oxygen?	Red
What are the proteins found on RBCs that carry oxygen called?	Hemoglobin
What are WBCs found in the lymph nodes called?	Lymphocytes
What are two types of WBCs?	**Lymphocytes and leukocytes**

Reproductive System

What is a gamete?	A sex cell (male or female)
Is the majority of the female reproductive system external or internal?	Internal
What does the female gamete travel down to reach the uterus?	Fallopian tube
What does a fertilized egg attach itself to?	The uterine wall
What is the inverted pear shaped muscular organ of the female reproductive?	Uterus
What is another name for the uterine wall?	Endometrium
What is the circular organ in the uterus that nourishes the fetus?	Placenta
What is the hormone secreting structure that develops in an ovary after it has been discharged from the fallopian tube?	Corpus luteum

Which glands produce testosterone and sperm?		Testes
What is the duct that receives sperm and moves from the testicles to the urethra?		Vas deferens
What are sperm cells and seminal fluid called?		Semen
What are the testes enclosed in?		Scrotum
What is the function of the bulbourethral gland?		To add a protein lubricant to the seminal fluid.

Hormone	Production Site	Function
Estrogen	Ovaries	Egg maturation
Luteinizing Hormone	Pituitary Gland	Egg Release
Progesterone	Corpus luteum (in ovary)	Regulates menstrual cycle and maintains pregnancy
Testosterone (Male/female hormone)	Male-Testes Female-Ovaries & adrenal glands	Male-develops male reproductive tissues, male physical characteristics, and sexual drive. Female- bone strength, brain function, muscle development, and sexual drive.

Where is the bulbourethral gland?	It is a pea shaped gland located beneath the prostate gland.
What is the j-shaped tube connected to the testicle that passes sperm to the vas deferens?	Epididymis
List examples of secondary sexual characteristics.	Fat deposits, muscle growth, mammary glands, facial hair.

Retinal Detachment

Will clients experience pain if the retina is detaches?	No, this is painless.
Is this a serious condition?	Yes, this is an emergency.
What are the signs of a detached retina?	Blurred vision, floaters, flashes of light, black spot
What is the treatment for a detached retina?	Surgery to reattach the retina.
What are the nursing interventions?	Cover both eyes with patches. No coughing, sneezing, strict bedrest keep head of bed elevated.

Reye's Syndrome

What is this condition?	Acute encephalopathy (brain disease).
Which other organs are involved?	Liver and kidneys.
What is the cause?	Usually, a viral infection. There is a link that when aspirin is used to treat a virus reye's syndrome will develop.
What is the treatment?	These clients usually end up in ICU for monitoring and treatment.

Respiratory Syncytial Virus

What organ is usually affected by RSV?

It passes through the nose and throat and enter the lungs.

How can RSV be transmitted?

Contact with nasopharyngeal droplet of a person with RSV, when coughing or sneezing. Also, by touching contaminated surfaces.

How many days is the incubation period of RSV?

4 to 6 days after exposure to the virus.

Can the virus remain alive on surfaces for hours?

Yes, it can remain alive on hard surfaces for few hours.

What are the main symptoms of RSV?

Coughing, runny nose, sneezing, wheezing, fever.

Can RSV cause complications?

Yes, RSV can lead to more serious condition like pneumonia, bronchiolitis, and otitis media.

Can we have RSV more than once?

Yes, RSV can infect a person more than once in a lifetime and even more than once in a single RSV season. Repeated infections are usually less severe than the first.

Are antibiotics given to RSV?

Antibiotics are not a therapy option for viral infections like RSV. The doctor may prescribed medications if testing reveals bacterial pneumonia or another infection.

Rheumatoid Arthritis

True or false? Rheumatoid arthritis is chronic.

True, this is a systemic inflammatory disease that affects the joints.

What are other clinical symptoms associated with rheumatoid arthritis?

Fatigue, weight loss, low-grade fever.

What are the 7S's of rheumatoid arthritis?

Sunrise stiffness
Soft feeling in the joints
Swelling in the joint
Symmetrical
Synovium (inflamed)
Systemic symptoms
Stages (synovitis, pannus, ankylosis)

Is there a particular age group that is affected?

No, it can occur at any age.

What factor will be found in the blood of a client with this form of arthritis?

Rheumatoid factor

___ ___ ___ will also be elevated in the blood

Erythrocyte sedimentation rate

Which joints are mostly affected?

Joints in the hands, wrists, feet, elbows, shoulders.

Will these joints be affected unilaterally or bilaterally?

Bilaterally - both hands, feet, and knees, etc.

Due to inflammation of the synovial membranes, which damages cartilage, joint _____ are seen.

Deformities

_____ are the primary drug therapy.

NSAIDS

What is the surgical intervention?	It is called arthrodesis. This is a joint fusion where 2 bones are united at a joint. Also a synovectomy-surgical removal of the synovia to help maintain joint function.
What are the treatments during flare ups?	REST-the joints are inflamed Heat treatment-for stiffness Cold treatment-for pain to help reduce the inflammation.
Should you encourage this client to exercise?	Yes, activity helps with the pain.

Rhinitis Pharyngitis, Tonsillitis, and Adenoiditis Laryngitis

Is laryngitis common to adults or children?	Children.
What type of precaution measure for streptococcal pharyngitis (tonsillitis)?	Droplet precaution.
How many feet away from the client should be observed when taking droplet precautions?	3 feet.
When a client is post tonsillectomy, what is the immediate observation to be considered?	Frequent swallowing (signs of bleeding).
What is the clinical manifestation of "Strep Throat"?	A fiery red pharyngeal membrane and fever.
What is the common finding for acute and chronic laryngitis?	Reinke's edema.
What is adenoiditis?	It occurs when there is inflammation of the adenoid tissue.
What is rhinitis?	When a reaction occurs that causes nasal congestion, runny nose, sneezing, and itching.
What is pharyngitis?	Commonly known as "sore throat" is an inflammation of the pharynx, resulting in a sore throat.
What causes tonsillitis?	Bacterial ex. group a strep. Viral.

SBAR Communication Technique

What does SBAR mean?	Situation, Background, Assessment & Recommendation.
Why is SBAR important?	It provides a framework for communication between members of the health-care team about a patient's condition.

S	Identify the Situation	Identify self, unit, patient name, room number. Identify admitting physician if speaking to the resident on call if speaking to the resident or intern. Briefly state the presenting problem. What it is, time of onset, and severity.
B	Describe the Background	Admitting diagnosis, recent surgeries, code status Vital signs and pertinent assessment data. Medications, allergies, IV fluids, lab and diagnostic test results.
A	Describe Assessment of the situation	What do you see? What is your impression? Examples may include allergic reaction, bleed, infection, MI, etc.
R	Present Recommendation on what you would like:	Patient needs to be seen now. Order change or new orders Physician input.

 Study more at ReMarNurse.com | Join live weekly on YouTube @ReMarNurse

Scabies

What are the most common symptoms?	Itching and rash
Where is the itching located?	Between the fingers, wrist, around the waist, and genitals. The head and neck are usually affected. Itching is increased at nite.
Does a client with scabies require isolation?	Yes, they should be placed under contact isolation.
What is the treatment?	Permethrin 5% Lindane
What nursing education should be included?	Treat all family members at same time. Wash all bed linens in hot water. Itching may occur a few weeks after treatment.

Schizophrenia

What is schizophrenia?	Schizophrenia is a group of mental disorders characterized by psychotic features (hallucinations and delusions) disordered thought processes, and disrupted interpersonal relationships
What are the positive symptoms?	Bizzare behavior, delusions, disorganized speech, hallucinations
What are the negative symptoms?	Blunted affect, inability to experience joy or pleasure (anhedonia) loss of motivation (avolition) Poverty of thought (alogia).
What are the cognitive symptoms?	Illogical thinking Impaired judgment Impaired memory Easily distracted Poor decision Poor problem solving skills
What are the depressive and other mood symptoms?	Dysphoria, hopelessness, suicidal thoughts.
What type of symptom is repeating the speech of another?	Echolalia
What type of symptom is repeating the movement of another?	Echopraxia
What type of symptom is holding a certain body position for hours?	Waxy flexibility
For clients with hallucinations what is the first priority?	For clients with hallucinations SAFETY is the first priority. Ensure that the client does not have any auditory command telling him or her to harm self or others.
What antipsychotic medications are effective for positive and negative symptoms?	Typical antipsychotics are more effective for positive signs of schizophrenia. Examples: Chlorpromazine, fluphenazine, haloperidol, Atypical antipsychotics are more effective for negative symptoms of schizophrenia Examples: clozapine, Lurasidone, olanzapine.

 Study more at ReMarNurse.com | Join live weekly on YouTube @ReMarNurse

Seizure Precautions

If the client has a seizure, what is the main goal?

To keep the client safe.

True or false? The nurse should mark the time and note client's behavior.

True.

Should the nurse restrain a client during seizures?

No, do not restrain

What should be done to a client during a seizure?

Turn head to the side, lie the bed flat, pad the head with pillow.

Should anything be put in the client's mouth to prevent the client from swallowing his/her tongue?

No, never do this.

Sepsis

What are the common causes of sepsis?

Bacterial, viral, or fungal infection

What are the risk factors that will lead to sepsis?

Weak immune system
Adults 65 or older
Having diabetes or cirrhosis
Wounds or injuries such as burns
children younger than one.

What are common clinical symptoms?

Generalized body swelling
Fever and chills
Difficulty in breathing
Mental confusion
Hyperventilation

Is sepsis contagious?

No

Is the heart rate fast or slow?

Tachycardia is present

Do the platelets increase or decrease?

There is a decrease in platelet count

Sexually Transmitted Disease (STDs)

	Chlamydia	Genital/Oral Herpes	Syphilis
Type of Infection	Bacteria	Virus	Bacteria
Incubation Period	1-3 weeks	3-7 days	Usually 3 weeks -Can range from 9 days to 3 months
Symptoms	Having no signs is common Female: vaginal discharge, lower abdominal pain, burning with urination Male: Urethritis	Urethral discomfort Lesions on vagina Or male genitalia The virus can be transmitted even when no sores are present if the client is shedding the virus.	Primary: chancres Secondary: fever, weight loss, rash
Treatment:	Penicillin	Acyclovir	Doxycycline

	Gonorrhea	Human Papilloma
Type of Infection	Bacteria	Virus
Incubation Period	Men: 3-30 days Women: 3 to indefinite	3-7 days
Symptoms	Men: urethritis, dysuria, burning yellow or green discharge Female: Yellow discharge, abdominal pain, bleeding with intercourse.	Genital warts on male and female genitalia
Treatment	Penicillin	No cure

Shingles (Herpes Zoster)

This viral infection is caused by which virus?

Varicella

What are the signs of herpes zoster?

Itching vesicles grouped together on top of a red rash, painful to touch, low-grade fever, malaise

How are shingles spread?

The vesicles contain fluid that transmits the virus.

Where is the rash usually located?

Along a dermatome.

What is a dermatome?

An area of skin that gets all of its innervations by a single spinal nerve.

What are some areas of dermatomes?

Face, trunk, back

Will the rash and vesicles be unilateral or bilateral?

Unilateral

What are the isolation precautions for Herpes Zoster?

Respiratory isolation

What is the treatment for shingles?

Analgesics
Supportive care
Cool compresses
Try to keep vesicles intact

What may be seen after the vesicles have healed?

Scarring.

Sickle Cell Anemia

Is this autosomal trait recessive or dominant?

Recessive; most commonly seen in African Americans.

How is this condition inherited?

A child receives the gene from both parents.

How long do sickled RBCs live compared to normal RBCs?

6-20 days; normal is 120.

What does this put the client at risk for?

Anemia

Which test determines sickle cell anemia?

Hemoglobin which shows anemia sickle testing of blood.

The acute exacerbation of sickle cell anemia is called ___ ____ ____.

Sickle cell crisis or a vaso-occlusive crisis.

The most common cause is _____.

Dehydration

This causes the sickled blood to do what?

Clot

What is the treatment of a sickle cell crisis?

Hydrate with oral and IV fluids. Give oxygen to increase tissue perfusion; a blood transfusion may be needed; give pain meds as this is a very painful condition.

During a sickle cell crisis, which intervention is done first-give oxygen or hydrate with IV fluids?

Hydrate with IV fluids; remember, during a crisis the blood is clumped together, so the goal is to decrease the viscosity of the blood. Oxygen will not reverse the cause; it will only prevent more clumping.

Skeletal System

What is a bone?	Calcified material that make up the skeleton.
What is hematopoiesis?	Production of blood cells.
What are the 4 major bone types?	Long, short, flat irregular.
What is an example of a long bone?	Humerus
What provides nutrients to bones?	Blood vessels
What is the fibrous sheath covering bones?	Periosteum
What is the tubular structure that synthesis the bones?	Osteon
What is cartilage?	Strong connective tissue in the body.
Which bone supports the tongue and is not connected to any other bone?	Hyoid bone
What is a Haversian canal?	Channels in the center of the bone that contain blood vessels and nerves.
What is another name for Haversian canal?	Central
Which canal communicates with the Haversian canal?	Volkmann canal
What is lamellae?	Layers or rings of bones or tissue.
What dense connective tissue attaches bone to bone?	Ligaments
What dense connective tissue attaches muscle to bone?	Tendons
What type of joints are responsible for movements?	Synovial joints
What is the viscous fluid found in the cavities of the synovial joints?	Synovial fluid
What are some examples of synovial joints?	1. Pivot 2. Ball & Socket 3. Hinge 4. Saddle
What is degenerative joint disease?	Osteoarthritis
What is an osteoblast?	Cells that make bone.
What is an osteocyte?	Mature bone cells.
What is an osteoclast?	Cells that remove bone.
What is a disease that causes brittle weak bones?	Osteoporosis

Starting an IV

1.	Inform client about procedure and indication.
2.	Gather supplies.
3.	Wash and dry hands.
4.	Use Universal Precautions - wear gloves
5.	Apply tourniquet.
6.	Locate a vein.
7.	Clean the area with alcohol.
8.	Position and insert needle, looking for a flash of blood.

Study more at ReMarNurse.com | Join live weekly on YouTube @ReMarNurse

9.	Advance catheter.
10.	Release the tourniquet.
11.	Remove the needle.
12.	Secure the catheter and start IV fluids if ordered.
13.	Document.

1.	Verify the doctor's order
2.	Gather all the necessary instruments, including the irrigation fluid and cup or syringe.
3.	Wash hands
4.	Explain the procedure to the client.
5.	Position the client: Have the client seated or lying down.
6.	Cover the Client's neck and shoulders with a waterproof sheet and towel.
7.	Tilt the Client's head toward the side being irrigated (to avoid infection of the opposite eye) and lean over a sink or kidney dish.
8.	Fill the irrigation cup with the irrigating solution and check the temperature by squeezing a small amount over the client's cheek.
9.	Instruct the client to direct his or her attention forward.
10.	Spread the eyelid, expose the lower conjunctival sac and keep the upper lid open with the non-dominant hand.
11.	Gently control the flow of solution along the conjunctival sac from the inner canthus to the outer canthus, onto the front surface of the eye and inside the lower and upper eyelids from no more than 5 centimeters.
12.	Ask the client to move their eyes continuously in all directions for at least 15 mins, preferably 30 mins, while irrigation is sustained.
13.	Using moist cotton buds or forceps, remove any remaining foreign bodies.
14.	Recheck the pH; if it stays unchanged or is not yet normal, continue with the irrigation.
15.	After the procedure is complete, check and record the client's visual acuity.

Sterile Technique

_____ can never be considered sterile, only clean.

Skin.

A nurse should never turn the _____ to a sterile field.

Back.

If a nurse has on a face mask and sterile gloves, is it okay to adjust the face mask with a gloved hand?

No, because once the gloves touch the mask they are no longer sterile.

A sterile gown is only sterile from the ____ to the ___.

Waist, shoulders

If a sterile wrapper becomes _____ the entire package is no longer sterile.

Wet

What is the purpose of the sterile technique?

To eradicate all potential microorganisms in and around a sterile environment while keeping items as free of microorganisms as possible.

What nursing procedures require sterile technique?

Procedures requiring sterile technique includes; inserting a urinary catheter, inserting an IV catheter, dispensing and administering IV drugs, and changing surgical dressings.

What is considered unsterile?

Unsterile means that it has not been properly sterilized, has come into contact with an item that is no longer regarded sterile, has entered a non-sterile field, or has reached the end of its shelf life.

| How long is the shelf life of a sterile item? | The shelf-life of a sterilized and packaged item is the amount of time that is deemed sterile. if the package is unopened it lasts up to one month. |

Why does the sterile field have to be dry?

Keep the sterile surface dry and replace it, if wet or broken. Any puncture, moisture, or break passing through a sterile barrier must be considered contaminated.

How are sterile solutions poured?

When pouring sterile liquids, just the lip and of the container are inner cap considered sterile. The pouring container must not contact any part of the sterile field. Splashes should be avoided.

Does jewelry have to be removed during sterile technique?

Yes, all dangling earrings, bracelets, necklaces, wristwatches, and rings should be removed before hand washing and wearing gloves. Microorganisms can live in jewelry.

How long hand washing should be?

Hand washing for roughly 20 seconds kills more germs from hands than washing for shorter periods.

How is clean technique different from sterile technique?

The purpose of the clean technique is to be free of marks and stains and limit the number of microorganisms wherever possible. The sterile procedure goes much further and eliminates any trace of bacteria or microorganisms by completely destroying microbes.

Suicidal Patient Assessment

General Guidelines	Provide a safe environment. Always take covert suicide threats seriously. Encourage expression of feelings. Do not argue with the patient. Show acceptance and appreciation
Lethality Assessment	**Intention:** Ask the patient if he or she thinks about or intends to harm self. **Plan:** Ask the patient if he or she has formulated a plan. What are the details: where, when, and how will the plan be carried out? **Means:** Check availability of method: access to gun, knife, pills, etc.? **Lethality of Means:** Pills vs. a gun, jumping vs. slitting wrist. Rescue: Is there a possibility of rescue.

Syndrome of Inappropriate Antidiuretic Hormone

What is SIADH?

A condition characterized by the excessive release of ADH.

What are the clinical signs of SIADH?

Fluid retention, oliguria, hyponatremia, this is because the body is unable to dilute the urine appropriately. Weakness

What are the causes of this condition?

Genetic disorder, surgery, medication induced, trauma, stroke, meningitis.

What are the characteristics of the urine?	It is concentrated urine, with increased urine specific gravity, decreased urine output.
Will there be cerebral changes?	Yes, mental status changes are expected, seizures can occur, increased intracranial pressure may be noted along with lethargy.
What are the diagnostic tests to be performed?	A physical exam-skin tugor, Mucous membranes and vital Sign checks. There is no specific diagnostic tool for SIADH
What is the treatment?	Find and treat the underlying cause. Correct the hyponatremia. Fluid restriction, loop or thiazide diuretics may be ordered. If a tumor is the cause it should be treated or removed.
What are the nursing interventions?	Monitor intake/output, daily weights, neurological checks, fluid status to check for edema. Instructing the client on fluid restriction to use hard candies, lozenges, moisturizing mouth swabs to combat dry mouth.

Systemic Lupus Erythematosus

What is the cause?	A defect in immunological mechanisms, with a genetic origin.
What type of rash does the client have if it's red in color and starts on the nose and expands to cheeks or face?	Malar rash (butterfly rash).
Is photosensitivity a clinical sign or not?	One of the major symptoms is photosensitivity.
Will the ESR and CRP levels be high or low?	Elevated erythrocyte sedimentation rate (ESR) and C-reactive protein level is observed to client with lupus (especially a flare).
What to monitor if a client is taking belimumab for a month?	Belimumab is a biologic that binds with a protein that supports the activity of B-cells. This decreases the antibody attacks and decreases inflammation. Depression and suicide are serious side effects of this medication.
Will the anti-nuclear antibodies (ANA) results be positive or negative?	Positive ANA (anti-nuclear) demonstrates that there are autoantibodies the body created against the nuclei of the dying cells.
What are the severe complications SLE?	Renal failure develops which leads to increased BUN/Creatinine, low urine output, proteinuria, weight gain, swelling in the upper & lower extremities.
What medication is used to treat SLE and decrease inflammation quickly, but it is not for long term use?	Prednisone is a steroid medication that is given.
What are the other side effects of prednisone?	Weight gain, susceptibility to diabetes and osteoporosis. Remember clients can also develop infections easily as well.

 Study more at ReMarNurse.com | Join live weekly on YouTube @ReMarNurse

Tardive Dyskinesia

This is a side effect of which medication?

Antipsychotics

What are the clinical signs?

A chewing motion with the mouth, tongue sticking in and out an involuntary movement of the arms and legs. Lip smacking, rapid eye blinking

Which class of medication can the nurse give to decrease these effects?

Anti-Parkinson's

Testicular Cancer

What is the cause?

A history of cryptorchidism (an undescended testicle) and genetic predisposition.

What is the way to detect this condition early?

By a monthly TSE (Testicular Self Examination) It should be done the same day each month. It is BEST after a shower.

What are the common symptoms of testicular cancer?

A painless testicular swelling a "dragging" or "pulling" sensation a palpable mass.

What are the late signs?

Back, bone pain, and respiratory symptoms.

What procedure is used to describe the stage?

Retroperitoneal lymph node dissection to stage the disease & reduce tumor volume.

When should the nurse notify the health care provider?

If the client feels any lumps, swelling or mass.

What type of surgical treatment is needed if prescribed by the physician?

Orchiectomy is a surgical procedure to remove one or both testicles.

The nurse needs to instruct the client post orchiectomy to avoid?

Avoid heavy lifting and strenuous activity.

A testicular self-examination should be done when?

After taking a warm shower.

Therapeutic Relationships

Who is involved?

The nurse and client. The client may invite caregivers if necessary.

How is a therapeutic relationship different?

A therapeutic relationship only focuses on the needs of the client.

What are the components involved?

Trust, genuine interest, empathy, acceptance, positive regard, self-awareness, & therapeutic use of self.

What is positive regard?

A nonjudgmental attitude that implies respect. For example; calling a client by name and openly and actively listening.

What are the 3 phases of the relationship?

1. Orientation
2. Working
3. Termination

What happens during the orientation phase?

The nurse and client meet.
Roles are established.
Questions are asked.
The nurse also discusses termination here.

The nurse has to tell the client she must report any harmful or dangerous behavior or comments. This is called a _____ to _____.

Duty to warn.

What happens during the working phase?	Problems are identified. Feelings are explored. Goals are set.
During the working phase transference can happen with the nurse. What is transference?	Client transfers feelings they have for significant others or parents to the nurse assisting them.

Torch Syndrome

What is TORCH?	**T**oxoplasmosis **O**thers (Syphilis or Hep B) **R**ubella **C**ytomegalovirus (CMV) **H**erpes simplex
What does TORCH mean in pregnancy?	This is a group of infectious diseases that affect a fetus or newborn baby.
What are the clinical signs?	Difficulty feeding, small areas of bleeding under the skin, small red or purple spots, hepatosplenomegaly.
Are TORCH infections contagious?	Yes, they are contagious.
How is TORCH diagnosed?	Through a blood test and viral culture.
How is TORCH treated?	Treatment for TORCH infections depend on the disease. Antibiotics, antivirals, and antiparasitic may be prescribed.
What are the prevention methods to teach?	Avoid contact with the ill. Wash hands often. Do not share drinks or food. Eat fully cooked meat and eggs. Avoid cleaning cats litter boxes. Wear condoms during sex.

The Transgender Client

How should the nurse address this client?	Ask them what they would like to be called.
If a male completes sexual reassignment surgery will she need a Pap smear exam?	No. Cervical pap smears are necessary as there will be no cervix in place.
If a female completes sexual re-assignment surgery will testicles be formed?	Yes. There will be testicles but they will not produce sperm.
Nursing considerations:	Nurses should tell the client in advance if they will have to expose their body to healthcare providers

Tracheostomy

What is a tracheostomy?	A surgical procedure that creates an open airway in the trachea.
What are the indications for a tracheostomy?	Upper airway obstructions.
What is the surgically created opening called?	A stoma.
What must the nurse always have at the bedside?	An obturator, a stiff plastic device used for inserting the inner cannula.
Is suctioning a client with a trach a clean or sterile procedure?	Sterile.
What should the nurse always do before suctioning a client with a trach?	Hyperoxygenate with 100% oxygen.

Should suction be applied during insertion of catheter?	No, this can cause damage to the client.
What should the nurse always do after suctioning a client with a trach?	Reoxygenate with 100% O2 2-3 times during inhalation.
If a client coughs strongly and the trach becomes dislodged, what are the initial nursing actions?	Keep the airway open by reinserting the obturator, then another inner cannula can be placed. Retention sutures can also be used. Give oxygen if the airway is lost!
If a client is NOT on a ventilator but has a trach, should the inner cuff be inflated?	No, it should be deflated not to block the airway.

Trigeminal Neuralgia

What is trigeminal neuralgia?	Sensory disorder that affects the 5th cranial nerve.
What are the risk factors of trigeminal neuralgia?	Herpes zoster, history of multiple sclerosis, age over 50 years, disorder of blood vessels, female gender, arteriovenous malformation.
What are the common complications of trigeminal neuralgia?	Weight loss, social isolation, loss of corneal reflex.
What are the common signs and symptoms of trigeminal neuralgia?	Remember PAINED in the FACE! **P**ain on the lips, face & gums. **A**long the trigeminal nerve. **I**nitiated by light touch. **N**o impairment of sensory or motor function. **E**xacerbated by extreme temperatures. **D**oes not shave or chew on the affected side. **F**avors the affected side, splinting affected side. **A** draft or cold air can aggravate it. **C**old drinks and food can aggravate. **E**ating, smiling, talking, and brushing teeth can exacerbate the pain.
What are the laboratory findings of trigeminal neuralgia?	Skull radiography, computed tomography, scanning (brain), and magnetic resonance imaging rule out sinus or tooth infections and tumors.
What is the major clinical manifestations of trigeminal neuralgia?	Severe facial pain.
What do you need to educate clients with trigeminal neuralgia?	Instruct the client to avoid hot or cold food. Instruct client to chew on unaffected side. Administer anticonvulsants as ordered. Prepare for microvascular decompression surgery if indicated.
Which is the correct diet small frequent feedings or a liquid diet?	Small frequent feedings of soft food.
What to avoid?	Hot soups or drinks, spicy food, sweets, caffeinated drinks, junk foods, processed foods.
What are things you need to remember about trigeminal neuralgia?	Remember NEURALGIA! **N**ature of pain **E**ye care **U**naffected side **R**oom temperature **A**ssess nature of pain **L**uke warm food hy**G**iene (oral) **I**ncrease protein & calories **A**void touching client.

Trimethoprim-Sulfamethoxazole

What is this medication used for?

To treat bacterial infections, most commonly UTIs.

What are the contraindications for this medication?

Kidney or liver failure

The severe inflammatory skin disorder caused by an allergic reaction to the medication is?

Steven-Johnson syndrome

What should clients be taught are expected side effects of this medication?

Photosensitivity, diarrhea, nausea loss of appetite, headache

What are the clinical signs of an allergic to this medication?

Severe skin lesions, blisters, swelling of throat, lips, tongue, fever; headache; rash *lesions can be internally on organs as well.

Tuberculosis (TB)

What organism is the cause of TB?

Mycobacterium tuberculosis.

What are the signs of active TB?

Productive cough, night sweats, chills, weight loss, low-grade fever.

The _____ test is administered by injecting a small amount of tuberculin intradermally.

Mantoux, also called PPD.

The Mantoux test is considered positive if the induration (raised skin) is greater than _____ mm.

10

What are the appropriate isolation precautions?

Airborne

The client's negative pressure room should have _____ fresh air exchanges per hour.

6

S.T.R.I.P.E. is the mnemonic for TB antibiotics. What are those medications?

STreptomycin
Rifampin
Isoniazid
Pyrazinamide
Ethambutol

What is the most common side effect of TB antibiotics?

Peripheral neuritis

What are the other side effects?

Muscle ache, GI disturbances, dizziness.

What colors will rifampin turn urine, sweat, and tears?

Red or orange

When taking TB antibiotics, which vitamin will be depleted?

B6

Teach the client to avoid _____ to reduce the risk of hepatotoxicity.

Alcohol

Clients taking TB antibiotics are at risk for _____ _____ hepatitis.

Drug-induced

How many consecutive sputum cultures need to be negative for the client to be non-contagious?

3

Ulcerative Colitis

What is the cause of this disease?	The cause is unknown.
What is the pathophysiology?	Inflammatory bowel disease affecting large intestine and rectum.
What are the signs or complaints from clients?	Abdominal pain, bloody diarrhea (20 stools/day), nausea, vomiting, and weight loss.
How is ulcerative colitis diagnosed?	Colonoscopy
What are the treatments?	Corticosteroids to reduce inflammation, removal of large intestine and rectum
What will the client need after surgery?	Ileostomy
What is the most appropriate diet for this condition?	A low fiber diet. Teach clients to avoid. Fiber which increase diarrhea. Fat or greasy foods also to decrease diarrhea. Teach clients to avoid alcohol (ETOH) and caffeine, but increase the fluid intake.

Urinary Tract Infection (UTI)

What is a urinary tract infection (UTI)?	An abnormal growth of bacteria in the urinary tract.
What is the most common causative bacteria?	Escherichia coli.
What are the clinical findings?	Urinary frequency/urgency dysuria, incontinence, cloudy foul-smelling urine, suprapubic tenderness
What are additional signs in the elderly?	Mental status change, fatigue, delirium.
What are the diagnostic exams?	Urinalysis, urine culture.
Who are the high-risk population groups?	Sexually active women, pregnancy, diabetes mellitus, indwelling catheters.
What are the treatment methods?	Antibiotics.

Uterine Displacement / Cystocele / Urethrocele / Rectocele

Uterine displacement is also known as _____.	Uterine prolapse. It is a type of pelvic organ prolapse, where in the uterus abnormally descends down or is herniated to the vagina.
What is the difference between a cystocele and a urethrocele?	Cystocele and urethrocele are types of pelvic organ prolapse that occur as anterior vaginal wall prolapse. The difference is when the bladder or the urethra is already involved it is categorized as urethrocele.
How do we distinguish a rectocele?	A rectocele is another type of pelvic organ prolapse that occurs as posterior vaginal wall prolapse involving the rectum.
What is the cause of the pelvic organ prolapse?	A defective pelvic floor. The pelvic floor can be weakened or damaged due to vaginal delivery, obesity, aging, chronic straining, or targeted injury in the pelvic floor

What are the clinical manifestations of pelvic organ prolapse?

Clinical manifestations include pelvic or vagina fullness, a sense of organs falling out, bulging of organs through the vaginal opening, and dyspareunia. Constipation or incomplete defecation may be noted with rectocele.

When inspecting for pelvic organ prolapse, advise the client to be in _____ position.

Lithotomy position. To inspect and detect cystoceles apply a single-bladed speculum against the posterior vaginal wall and allow the client to strain. For the rectoceles, retract the anterior vaginal wall and instruct the client to strain.

_____ is non-surgical management of pelvic prolapse. It supports the vagina and it comes as a ring, doughnut, cube, or inflatable.

Vaginal pessary. It is inserted in the vagina maintaining proper placement and reducing prolapsed organs.

What exercise can be helpful to strengthen the pelvic muscle?

Kegel's exercise. Pubococcygeus muscles are contracted tightly for about 2 seconds, then relaxed for about 10 seconds. Upon repeat gradually increase the timing of contractions.

When is surgical repair intended?

Surgery is the last option of management since it can cause additional damage to the organs. However, if the client is severely symptomatic and conservative management was ineffective surgery is then indicated.

Vital Signs

What are the four main objective data?

Pulse rate, respiratory rate, blood pressure and body temperature.

What is considered the fifth vital sign?

Pain-this is always subjective data.

What are the routes of temperature measurement?

Axillary, oral, tympanic, rectal, temporal.

What does the temperature measure?

The warmth of the human body.

How is heat lost from the body?

The skin, lungs, body waste, convection, evaporation

What is thermoregulation?

The ability to maintain a stable body temperature.

Wilson's Disease

What is Wilson's disease?

It is a genetic defect that causes copper buildup in the body. The body is unable to remove extra copper.

What two organs are affected the most?

Liver and brain

What is the diet for this client?

Low copper

What foods are high in copper and should be avoided?

Lamb, shellfish, vegetable juice, nectarines, dried beans chocolate, and multi-vitamins.

PHARMACOLOGY SECTION

Featuring -The Top 250 Medications for Nursing School

Adrenergic Agonists

Drug	Selegiline	Epinephrine	Dopamine	Phenylephrine	Norepinephrine
Route	Oral, Transdermal	IV, IM	IV infusion	IV, Oral, Nasal	IV-infusion
Indications	Oral: Parkinson's disease Transdermal: Major depressive disorder	Cardiac Arrest Anaphylaxis Bronchospasm Mucosal bleeding Local vasopressin Anesthetics	Cardiogenic shock Septic shock Bradycardia Hypotension Heart block	Hypotension Nasal Congestion Priapism	Cardiogenic shock Kidney disease Post cardiac arrest Septic shock
Side Effects	Dizziness Dry mouth Headache Hypotension Chest pain Skin changes	Anxiety Hypertension Headache Tremor Palpitations Arrythmias	N & V HTN Arrythmias Azotemia Headache Chest pain, Palpitations vasoconstriction, dyspnea, Piloerection (goose bumps)	Rebound congestion esp. when used longer than 3 days. Mild CNS stimulation Nasal: Stinging Ophthalmic: Transient burning/ stinging	Bradycardia Cardiomyopathy, Peripheral vascular insufficiency Anxiety
Contraindications	Clients under the age of 12 due to increased risk of HTN crisis. Clients with Pheochromocytoma.	Clients with hypothyroidism may have an increased production of adrenergic receptors in the vasculature and can cause hypersensitive response.	Clients with pheochromocytoma, ventricular fibrillation. Hypersensitivity to sulfites. Ischemic heart disease Recent use of MAOIs, post-MI.	IV: Severe hypertension, ventricular tachycardia. Oral: Hyperthyroidism bradycardia, partial heart block, cardiac disease Cardiogenic shock, HTN.	Hypotension cases that are related to hypovolemia except in emergency to maintain coronary/cerebral perfusion until volume replaced.
Client Education Safety	To avoid sudden and severe hypertension, avoid foods rich in tyramine, dopamine, phenylalanine, tryptophan and caffeine. Monitor BP, mood, and behavior.	Epinephrine autoinjectors (*for anaphylaxis*) Advise client to carry the injector at all times since anaphylaxis is unpredictable. Store in an even temperature.	Low BP may happen if stopped abrupt. Do not use solutions darker than slightly yellow, brown, indicates decomposition. Use infusion pump to control flow rate.	Parents need to be instructed to be careful with the use of these drugs— they should check the labels for ingredients, monitor the recommended dose.	Teach client to report headaches, dizziness, and sudden changes in skin sensation. Assess EKG, BP continuously. Monitor IV flow rate diligently. Assess for extravasation of IV site extremity. Monitor I & O; report urine output less than 30 ml/hr.

Allergy Medications

Drug	Diphenhydramine
Classification	Antihistamine
Routes	PO, IV, IM
Use	Antihistamine for allergy relief Acute dystonic reaction relief Prevention of motion sickness
Action	Antagonizes the effects of histamine at H1 receptor sites. *This medication is a significant CNS depressant and anticholinergic.
Contraindications	Blurry vision, hypotension, anorexia are adverse effects. Wheezing, chest tightness indicates an allergic reaction. Do not give to patients with bladder neck obstructions, narrow angle glaucoma.
Client Education	May cause drowsiness, do not drive while taking. May cause dry mouth due to anticholinergic effect. Educate the patient on the use of sunscreen and protective clothing as photosensitivity reactions may occur. Educate the patients on not to use alcohol or other CNS depressants while taking this medication.

Drug	Cetirizine -Fexofenadine -Loratadine
Classification	Antihistamines
Route	PO
Use	Temporarily relieve the symptoms of hay fever and allergies to pollen, dust, animal dander, and other substances.
Action	Selectively antagonizes peripheral histamine H1 receptors.
Contraindications	Do not give to children under the age of 2. Avoid in clients with renal impairment. Assess respiratory status such as wheezing or chest tightness.
Client education	Drug interactions may occur if given with benzodiazepines, cough medicines, or other antihistamines. May cause drowsiness, do not operate heavy machinery until the patient knows how the drug will affect them. Do not take with alcohol. Stop 48 hours before an allergy test.

Drug	Beclomethas<u>one</u>	Fluticas<u>one</u>	Mometas<u>one</u>	Triamcinol<u>one</u>
Route	Nasal Sprays			
Use	Rhinitis Chronic asthma Nasal polyps These are corticosteroids which have an anti-asthmatic effect as well.			
Action	Prevents inflammation by the suppression of leukocytes and fibroblasts.			
Contraindications	Avoid if clients have a history of angioedema, renal insufficiency, and bronchospasms.			
Client education	Patients may be at risk for fungal infections. Teach the patient to report vision changes			

Analgesics

Drug	Acetaminophen	Naproxen	NSAIDs	Aspirin (ASA)
Route	PO, Suppository, IV	PO	PO	PO
Uses	Mild to moderate pain, fever, headache	Mild to moderate pain, decreases inflammation, reduce fever	Mild to moderate pain, fever, rheumatoid arthritis, osteoarthritis.	Inhibits platelet aggregation, reduces inflammation, temporary pain relief of headache, pain, and fever.
Action	Inhibits the synthesis of prostaglandins that may serve as mediators of pain and fever.	Inhibition of cyclo-oxygenase, which in turn reduces prostaglandin synthesis	Blocks cyclooxygenase (or COX) used by the body to make prostaglandins.	Inhibits platelet aggregation, has antipyretic analgesic
Contraindications	Chronic alcohol use/abuse Hepatic disease A history of hypersensitivity.	A history of peptic ulcers. Hypertension or heart failure. ETOH abuse as this can increase bleeding. Do not give with garlic, ginseng, or ginkgo biloba.	GI bleeding Hepatotoxicity Do not give to clients taking low dose aspirin. Patients with a Vit K deficiency May cause hyperkalemia.	May cause GI bleeding, do not give to clients with hypersensitivity
Client Education	Assess for pain and fever relief. Overdose poisoning is possible. The antidote is N-acetylcysteine.	Take this medication with food. Teach the client that GI upset and bleeding	May increase the risk of bleeding with warfarin, heparin. May increase risk of bleeding. Teach patient to take NSAIDs with food or milk. May cause photosensitivity.	Take this medication with a full glass of water or milk. Remain in an upright position 15-30 mins after administration. Advise the client to report tinnitus, unusual bleeding of gums, or black, tarry stools.

Drug	Morphine	Hydromorphone	Codeine	Meperidine hcl	Oxycodone
Route	PO, IV	IM, IV, subcutaneous, rectal, or PO.	PO	IM, Subcutaneous, IV, syrup, and tablet.	IM, IV, Subcutaneously, rectal
Uses	To relieve severe pain	Manages moderate to severe pain and chronic pain	A reduction of a non-productive cough.	Reduces moderate to severe pain. Used as obstetric analgesia	Moderate to severe pain
Action	Morphine is a selective mu agonist that produces analgesia and sedation.	Opioid agonist	Selective mu receptor but with a weaker affinity than morphine	A Kappa-opiate receptor agonist	The full mechanism is unknown. Activation of mu opioid receptors inhibit responses to pain.
Contradictions	Acute asthma Paralytic ileus Hepatic failure	Caution with benzodiazepines/other CNS depressants may cause severe sedation.	Should not be given to children under 12.	Do not give to patients who have taken an MAOI in the last 14 days. Do not take with alcohol. Avoid in clients with head injuries. Do not give to clients with asthma.	Hypersensitivity Alcoholism, renal/liver disease Addison's disease
Client Education	Respiratory depression may occur. May cause drug addiction. Naloxone is the antidote. Severe constipation is expected orthostatic hypotension can occur.	Respiratory depression, and hypotension should be assessed. May cause dizziness, lightheadedness, and fainting change positions slowly. Constipation is an expected side effect. This may cause addiction. Naloxone is an antidote.	May cause respiratory depression. This medication may cause adrenal gland issues. May be habit forming. Naloxone is an antidote.	Respiratory depression. SC route can be painful. May cause bronchoconstriction in newborn. Do not use with St. John's wort. Naloxone is an antidote.	Respiratory depression, dizziness, sedation may cause hepatotoxicity when combined with acetaminophen. Naloxone is an antidote.

Antibiotics

Drug	Aminoglycosides	PCN	Tetracyclines	Cephalosporins	Ciprofloxacin	Fluoroquinolones
Route	PO, IV, Inhalation Intraperitoneal Intraventricular	PO PCN G: IM, IV PCN V: PO	PO, Topical Ophthalmic	PO, IV, IM	PO, IV Otic Ophthalmic	PO, IV
Indications	Infective endocarditis Sepsis Complicated intraabdominal infections Complicated genitourinary infections.	Pneumonia Staphylococcal infections Bacterial Endocarditis Syphilis Anthrax Diphtheria Rat-Bite Fever Whipple's disease	Pneumonia Upper respiratory tract infection Chlamydia PID Syphilis Traveler's diarrhea Lyme disease Legionnaire's disease	Skin and skin-structure infections, Bone infections Genitourinary infections Otitis media Community-acquired respiratory tract infections	UTI STDs Skin and tissue infections Bone, joint infections Prostatitis Pneumonia Typhoid fever Lower respiratory tract infections	Bacterial bronchitis Pneumonia Septicemia Joint and bone infections Soft tissue and skin infections Typhoid fever Urethral infections PID
Side Effects	Ototoxicity Trouble maintaining balance. Paralysis of skeletal muscles Skin rash Alopecia Anorexia Nephrotoxicity,	Allergic reaction Diarrhea Flu symptoms Easy bruising Urinating less Agitation confusion unusual thoughts Seizure	N/V Diarrhea Itching of the rectum or vagina Swollen tongue Black or hairy tongue Sore throat Headache Blurred vision Skin rash Hives Edema Joint stiffness	Stomach upset N/V Diarrhea Yeast infection Oral thrush Dizziness Watery diarrhea Abdominal pain Fever Nausea Decreased appetite.	N/V Stomach pain Heartburn Diarrhea Vaginal itching Sleepiness Rash Hives, Itching Peeling of skin Fever Edema Hoarseness sweating Chest pain Urinary changes	Drowsiness Tendon pain Painful joints Abnormal pain or sensations e.g., pins and needles, tingling, tickling or burning Severe tiredness Anxiety Depression Poor memory
Contra-indications	Hypersensitivity Myasthenia Gravis	Hypersensitivity Steven-Johnson Syndrome	Pregnant Hypersensitivity Children under age of 8	Neonates with hyper-bilirubinemia	Hypersensitivity tizanidine for muscle spasms Myasthenia gravis	Hypersensitivity Myasthenia gravis Warfarin, mineral supplements Pregnancy Breast-feeding Seizures Cardiovascular, hepatic, or renal disease.
Client Education Safety	Monitor serum BUN/ creatinine. Cochlear function during toxicity. These medications are inactivated by PCN.	Teach patient to complete the entire course of treatment. Watch for signs of superinfections: black furry growth on tongue, vaginal itching, loose stools.	May cause skin photosensitivity. Avoid too much sun exposure. Use sunscreen, sunglasses, and protective clothes. If used in children age 8 and below can result in persistent tooth discoloration.	Do not drink alcohol while on cephalosporins to avoid disulfiram-like reactions. May increase the risk of bleeding. Monitor nephrotoxicity. Complete the entire course of antibiotics, even if symptoms have subsided.	Ciprofloxacin may cause QT prolongation. Alcohol and marijuana use may increase risks of dizziness. Ciprofloxacin may affect blood sugar level. Check blood sugar regularly and report the result to the doctor.	Have a total of fluid intake of 1500mL-2000mL per day while taking the medication, unless contraindicated. Avoid medications with calcium, aluminum, iron, or zinc because it may impair absorption of the drug, Monitor for photosensitivity

Anticoagulants

	Heparin	Warfarin
Onset	Less than one hour	4-10 days
Short term or Long term?	Short term	Long term
Routes	IV or SQ	PO only
Labs to watch	PTT PTT should be 1.5-2.5 times the control	INR or PT INR should be 2-3.
Antidote	Protamine sulfate	Vitamin K
Pregnancy Safe	Yes, you can give	No, don't give, there is a baby in there!
Will this medication break down a clot?	No	No
Potential complications of the drug therapy	Heparin induced thrombocytopenia (HIT)	Coumadin induced necrosis

	Enoxaparin
Indication	Prevent deep vein thromboses (DVT), Post-surgical blood thinner. Used to treat/prevent the complications of angina.
Route	Subcutaneous injection or IV (less common) Injections are given for a total of 10-14 days.
Assessment	Medication should be clear with no particles or discoloration before injecting. Monitor for signs of bleeding.
Contraindications	Do not give if client has a history of heparin-induced thrombocytopenia. Avoid in patients with GI bleeding, thrombocytopenia. Clients should stop taking 24 hours before surgery. Do not administer with other blood thinners.
Client Education	This is considered a *Low Molecular Weight Heparin (LMWH)* The benefits of LMWH over Heparin: Once daily injections. No lab monitoring. This can be prescribed as outpatient therapy. The client should monitor for signs of bleeding.

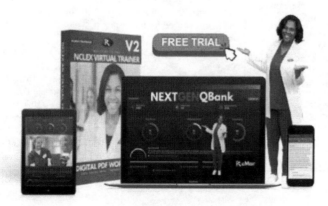

Antidepressants

Drug	Selective Serotonin Reuptake inhibitor	Serotonin & Norepinephrine Reuptake Inhibitor	Monoamine oxidase inhibitor	Tricyclic antidepressants
Route	Oral	Oral	Oral, Skin patch (rare)	Oral
Indications	Major depressive disorder Generalized anxiety disorder Bulimia nervosa Obsessive-compulsive disorder Panic disorder Post-traumatic stress disorder	Major depressive disorder Fibromyalgia Generalized anxiety disorder (GAD). Pain from diabetes-related neuropathy. Social anxiety disorder Panic disorder	Phenelzine Depression. Panic disorder. Social anxiety disorder Selegiline: Major depressive disorder. Parkinson's disease.	Major depressive disorder
Side Effects	Nausea, vomiting or diarrhea Headache Drowsiness Dry mouth Insomnia Nervousness, agitation Dizziness Sexual problems Weight changes	Nausea and vomiting. Dry mouth (xerostomia). Constipation. Fatigue and drowsiness. Dizziness. Excessive sweating Sexual dysfunction.	Dizziness or lightheadedness Hypotension Dry mouth Nausea. Diarrhea or constipation. Drowsiness. Insomnia.	Drowsiness Blurred vision Constipation Dry mouth Hypotension Urine retention Weight loss Diaphoresis Excessive sweating Sexual dysfunction
Contra-indications	Simultaneous use of MAOIs, linezolid, and other drugs that raise serotonin Paroxetine is not recommended for pregnant women due to its teratogenic effects in developing cardiovascular abnormalities, notably heart deformities, if taken during the first trimester.	Hypersensitivity Closed-angle glaucoma Severe hepatic and nephrotic impairment	Combining it with SSRIs increases the risk of serotonin syndrome, a possibly fatal. Tyramine, a substance found in wine and aged cheese, can trigger a hypertensive crisis when taken alongside MAOIs. Aged cheeses, red wine, beer, soy products, overripe bananas, and cured, smoked, aged, or pickled meats should all be avoided by patients using MAOIs.	With a family history of QTc interval prolongation or sudden cardiac death. Hypersensitivity reactions may occur.
Client Education Safety	SSRIs are not addictive. Gradually reduce dose to prevent rebound syndromes. Avoid alcohol use. If suicide ideation occurs discontinue. May cause more bleeding if used with NSAIDs or blood thinners.	Never discontinue taking an SNRI without first consulting the doctor. SNRI "withdrawal" is known as "antidepressant discontinuation syndrome."	MAOIs are normally not given to children, although anyone taking an antidepressant should be closely monitored for increasing depression or strange behavior. If any suicidal thoughts arise, immediately get medical attention or call for emergency assistance. Stopping MAOI abruptly is more likely to result in discontinuation syndrome.	Individuals with documented cardiac problems, careful monitoring of cardiac function, electrocardiogram (ECG), and blood pressure is essential. To reduce the risk of developing arrhythmias, clients with low potassium blood concentrations should be monitored on a regular basis.

Antidiabetics

Classification	Sulfonylureas	Meglitinides	Biguanides	Thiazolidinediones
Generic Names	Glipizide Glyburide Gliclazide Glimepiride Chlorpropamide Tolbutamide	Repaglinide Nateglinide	Metformin	Rosiglitazone Pioglitazone
Indications	Sulfonylureas bind to the beta cells found in the pancreas and increases insulin release.	Meglitinides act on the beta-cell receptors by regulating ATP-sensitive potassium channels leading to increased insulin production.	Biguanides boost hepatic activity, which reduces hepatic gluconeogenesis and lipogenesis and increases insulin-mediated glucose uptake in muscle cells.	Thiazolidinediones trigger peroxisome proliferator-activated receptor gamma, which activates insulin sensitivity and increases peripheral glucose uptake.
Side effects	Dizziness, GI Upset Nervousness Anxiety /Depression Pain, Paresthesia Headache , Pruritus Hypoglycemia	Hypoglycemia Weight gain Headache, GI upset Upper respiratory tract infection Cardiovascular ischemia	GI upset Nausea and vomiting Flatulence Chest discomfort, Sweating Palpitation Chills Dizziness, Taste disorder Vitamin B12 deficiency	Edema Hypoglycemia Cardiac failure Headache Bone fracture Myalgia Sinusitis/ Pharyngitis
Considerations Safety	Do not give if allergic to sulfa. Monitor kidney function. Do not mix up chlorpropamide with chlorpromazine (psych med) this could be deadly.	Rapid acting medications. Can be used in combination with metformin. All patients should be screened for Heart failure & Liver toxicity when taking this medication.	Less likely to cause hypoglycemia than the other medications. May cause lactic acidosis. Approved for children 10 years and older. Used in the treatment of women with PCOS	All patients should be screened for heart failure & liver toxicity when taking this medication.

Classification	Alpha Glucosidase inhibitors	DPP-4 inhibitors	SGLT2 inhibitors	GLP-1 receptors
Generic Names	Acarbose Miglitol Voglibose	Alogliptin Linagliptin Saxagliptin Sitagliptin	Dapagliflozin Canagliflozin	Semaglutide Liraglutide
Indications	Delay the absorption of glucose.	Prolongs the effect of increased insulin secretion by slowing the breakdown of GLP-1.	Promotes the loss of glucose in the urine. Prevents serum glucose from being absorbed.	Enhances glucose dependent insulin secretion by the beta cells.
Side Effects	Flatulence Diarrhea Abdominal pain Increased serum transaminases	Hypoglycemia Nasopharyngitis Acute pancreatitis Peripheral edema Headache	Dyslipidemia hyperphosphatemia Hypovolemia Nausea/Vomiting Renal impairment.	Delayed gastric emptying Constipation Decreased desire to eat *Pancreatitis Thyroid tumors
Considerations Safety	Severe liver toxicity can be noted. These do not increase insulin production. Used in combination with metformin or sulfonylureas.	Oral medications that decreases glucagon secretion. Monitor for low blood sugar. Also slows GI emptying. This is a combination medication with diet and exercise.	Patient is at risk for dehydration, hypotension and urinary tract infections. Monitor for bone loss as bone density may decrease.	Given in combination with oral medications. Should not be given if patient is unable to eat. These are SQ injections given once a week. Exenatide mimics the GLP 1 medications in action. This is a sq medication BID or once a week.

Antiemetics

Drug	Ondansetron	Promethazine	Meclizine
Route	IV or Oral	IM, Oral or Rectal	Oral
Indications	Chemotherapy -induced nausea and vomiting (N/V). Postoperative N/V Pregnancy / Vertigo -associated nausea and vomiting,	Allergic conditions Motion sickness Nausea/Vomiting May be used as a mild sedative.	Prevention/treatment of nausea, vomiting, vertigo due to motion sickness. Treatment of vertigo associated with diseases affecting the vestibular system.
Side Effects	Anxiety, dizziness, drowsiness Headache, fatigue Constipation or diarrhea Hypoxia Urinary retention Abdominal pain Xerostomia Fever Feeling of cold Redness/pain at injection site Paresthesia Hypersensitivity reaction Blurred vision	Drowsiness, dry mouth, nose, and throat Urinary retention Increased mucus production Epigastric distress Visual/ hearing disturbances Wheezing, paresthesia Diaphoresis, chills Disorientation Hypotension, confusion Syncope in elderly Photosensitivity Nightmares	Allergic reactions Drowsiness Blurred vision Dry mouth, nose, and throat Difficulty swallowing
Contra-indications	Hypersensitivity to ondansetron or any component of the formulation. Medication interactions: sotalol, quinidine, thioridazine, chlorpromazine may cause long QT intervals.	Contraindicated in children 2 years and younger may cause breathing to stop. May increase secretions in respirations caution in patients with asthma or COPD.	Hypersensitivity to meclizine or any component of the formulation. Do not administer with benzodiazepines as it may increase sedative effects. May make certain kinds of glaucoma worse. Clients with kidney disease.
Client Education **Safety**	Oral dosage forms should be taken 30 minutes prior to chemotherapy, 30- 60 minutes prior to surgery and 1- 2 hours prior to radiation therapy. May cause constipation. Monitor ECG for QT prolongation, electrolyte imbalances, heart failure, bradyarrhythmia, and serotonin syndrome.	Drowsiness, dry mouth may be expected. Avoid tasks that require alertness and motor skills until response to drug is established. Sugarless gum, sips of water may relieve dry mouth. Coffee, tea may help reduce drowsiness. Report visual disturbances, involuntary movements, restlessness. Avoid alcohol and other CNS depressants. Avoid prolonged exposure to sunlight.	This can decrease mental alertness. Ask clients to refrain from tasks that require alertness and motor skills until response to drug is established. Monitor blood pressure. Monitor children closely for paradoxical reactions. Monitor serum electrolytes in clients with severe vomiting. Assess hydration status of client

Antifungals

Antifungal Drug Classes	Examples	Indications	Nursing Considerations	Significant Adverse Effects
Polyenes	Amphotericin B (IV) Nystatin (oral)	Severe fungal infections Candidiasis of the oral esophageal.	Administer amphotericin slowly via IV infusion to minimize adverse reactions. For oral nystatin swish and swallow or swish and spit according to the order.	Infusion related reactions such as fever, chills, respiratory distress. Amphotericin B may cause severe renal impairment, bone marrow suppression, vomiting, and weight loss. Amphotericin B should not be used in pregnancy. Gastrointestinal discomfort.
Azoles	Ketoconazole Fluconazole Itraconazole	Candidiasis, cryptococcal meningitis, histoplasmosis, aspergillosis.	These medications block steroids and testosterone. Ketoconazole is available as a shampoo and cream.	These medications may cause liver and renal dysfunction. May further complicate fertility issues.
Echinocandins	Anidulafungin Caspofungin Micafungin	Invasive candidiasis Esophageal candidiasis	Anidulafungin may cross the placenta and enter breast milk All the medications can cause liver toxicity.	Monitor as bone marrow suppression can occur. Do not use cyclosporine with caspofungin.
Pyrimidine	Flucytosine	Systemic infections Cryptococcal infections	Monitor renal function Monitor potassium levels	Photosensitivity Leukopenia Aplastic anemias

General Education

These meds are very toxic when given systemically. Fungi differ from bacteria and have a rigid cell wall.
Some systemic fungal medications can be given for as long as 6 months for chronic infections.

Topicals Antifungals

These medications treat a variety of tinea infections.

Clotrimazole	Miconazole	Ketoconazole	Terbinafine	Tioconazole
Over the counter treatment for oral and vaginal candida infections.	Treatment of local, topical mycoses including bladder and vaginal infections and athlete's foot.	Treatment of seborrheic dermatitis, tinea corporis, tinea cruris, tinea pedis	Short term treatment of topical mycosis: treatment of tinea infections	Treatment of recurrent vaginal candida infections.

General Education about Antifungals:

When the antifungal medications are applied locally as a cream, lotion, or spray, effects include irritation, burning, rash, and swelling.
Do not use topicals longer than 6 weeks due to the risk of adverse effects and possible emergence of resistant strains of fungi.
Teach the client to use clean, dry socks when treating athlete's foot to help eradicate the infections.
The area of fungal infections should be cleaned with mild soap and water.

Antihyperlipidemics

Drug	Example	Indications	Nursing Considerations	Significant Adverse Effects
Statins (HMG CoA Reductase Inhibitors)	Atorvastatin Fluvastatin Lovastatin Rosuvastatin Simvastatin	1. Hypercholesterolemia 2. Mixed hyperlipidemia 3. Primary and secondary prevention of cardiovascular disease.	The maximum effect takes place when dietary cholesterol intake is at its lowest. Taking statins with underlying hypothyroidism could lead to rhabdomyolysis. Use with caution for clients with hepatic and renal impairment.	Headaches Gastrointestinal disturbances Muscle aches Elevated liver enzymes Rhabdomyolysis-patient will report muscle weakness.
Niacin (Nicotinic Acid)	Niaspan Slo-niacin	1. Familial hyperlipidemias 2. Severe hypercholesterolemias	The medication is effective in increasing high-density lipoprotein (HDL). The effect is maximized with regular exercise and diet modification to a low fat, high fiber diet.	Skin flushing Pruritus
Fibrates (Fibric acid)	Gemfibrozil Fenofibrate	1. Hypertriglyceridemia 2. Dysbetalipoproteinemia	Fibrates increase biliary cholesterol excretion leading to gallstone formation. Gemfibrozil is contraindicated with simvastatin use. Monitor for bleeding or easy bruising if the client is taking warfarin.	Gastrointestinal disturbances Myositis Use precaution in clients with renal impairment, hepatic dysfunction and gallbladder disease. It can lead to myopathy and rhabdomyolysis.
Bile Acid Sequestrants	Colesevelam Colestipol Cholestyramine	1. Type IIA and IIB hyperlipidemias	Cholestyramine relieves pruritus caused by the accumulation of the bile acids in clients with biliary stasis. Colesevelam is indicated for clients with diabetes mellitus because of its glucose-lowering effects. Bile acid sequestrants Impair the absorption of fat-soluble vitamins.	Constipation Nausea Flatulence *Teach the client to take fat-soluble vitamins 1 to 2 hours before or 4 to 6 hours after.
Cholesterol Absorption Inhibitor	Ezetimibe	Alternative for statin intolerant clients	Contraindicated in clients with moderate to severe hepatic insufficiency.	Uncommon
Omega Fatty Acids	Docosahexaenoic and eicosapentaeneoic acid Icosapent ethyl	Alternative for lipid-lowering therapies for clients with significantly elevated triglycerides (more than or equal to 500 mg/dl)	-Does not reduce cardiovascular morbidity and mortality. -Bleeding risk is higher for clients receiving anticoagulants and antiplatelets.	Abdominal pain Nausea Diarrhea

Antihypertensive Drugs

Drug	ACE Inhibitors	Arbs	Beta Blockers	Calcium Channel Blocker	Digoxin
Route	Oral, IV	Oral	Oral, IV, eye drops	Oral, IV	Oral, IV, IM
Indications	Hypertension Heart failure Coronary artery disease Post M.I. Diabetes mellitus Chronic kidney disease Glomerular disease	Hypertension Heart attack Heart failure Stroke Fatty liver disease Chronic kidney disease Diabetes mellitus	Cardiac arrhythmias Heart failure Hypertension Angina Glaucoma Peripheral artery disease Myocardial infarction	Hypertension Coronary artery disease Chest pain Arrhythmias Raynaud's disease Pulmonary hypertension Subarachnoid hemorrhage	Arrhythmias Heart failure
Side Effects	Dry cough Hyperkalemia Hypotension Fatigue Headaches. Dizziness Loss of taste. Elevated Creatinine and BUN	Dizziness Dry cough Metallic or loss of taste Skin rash Swelling of the skin Hyperkalemia Kidney failure	Lightheadedness Dizziness Weight gain Hyperglycemia Erectile dysfunction Nausea Constipation	Lightheadedness Dizziness Skin flushing Headache Swelling limbs Constipation GERD Arrhythmias Gingival hyperplasia Fatigue Nausea Diarrhea	Diarrhea, N &V dizziness, headache *Allergic reactions symptoms: skin rash, hives. Blurred vision Yellow-green tint vision Hallucinations Fainting Abdominal pain Fast, irregular heart rate
Contra-indications	Allergic reactions Pregnancy Breastfeeding History of angioedema Kidney disease Renal disorders Hypovolemia	Pregnancy Hyperkalemia Renal artery stenosis	Diabetic patients on insulin Asthmatic patients Kidney disease Pregnancy Breastfeeding Do not take with nitrates.	Heart failure 2nd or 3rd-degree heart block. Severe hypotension Acute M.I. Pulmonary congestion. Renal/Liver disease	Acute MI Allergic reactions Hypomagnesemia Hypokalemia Wolf-Parkinson-White syndrome Pregnant Breastfeeding
Client Education **Safety**	Call 9-1-1 if swelling, especially in the mouth, throat, or face can occur. Fainting, loss of consciousness, signs of a heart attack or stroke. Monitor CBC, electrolytes and renal function.	Check MD before taking medicines for allergies, coughs and colds, and NSAIDs. Some medication can cause an increase in blood pressure. ARBs may increase potassium levels.	Prolongs symptoms of hypoglycemia Bronchoconstriction in asthma patients Do not administer if systolic blood pressure less than 100.	Avoid grapefruit products which can cause dizziness and fainting. Do not consume alcohol as it interferes with the effectiveness.	Monitor BP and HR daily. Do not administer apical HR less than 60. Do not stop taking this medication abruptly. To prevent delayed absorption, take this drug at least 2 hours before or after consuming foods high in fiber.

Antihypertensive Drugs

Name	Nitroglycerin
Action	It is a vasodilator given to reduce preload and afterload of the heart.
Effects	It lowers blood pressure and increases the oxygenation of tissues.
Safety Contraindications	Do not take with sildenafil citrate. A client can take one or the other, but never both as it causes severe hypotension! When nitro SL, a nurse can give only up to three tablets over 15 minutes. Give one tablet every five minutes. Call emergency medical services after second tablet of nitroglycerin is given. Do NOT eat or drink while taking it. If giving nitroglycerin via a patch, never place over a pacemaker. First remove the patch before client goes into MRI. If the MD orders nitro IV, place on an infusion pump always!

Antineoplastics

Drug	Example	Indication	Side Effects	Client Education Safety
Taxanes	Paclitaxel Docetaxel Cabazitaxel	Ovarian cancer Breast cancer Nonsmall cell lung cancer Gastric cancers	Bronchospasm Cardiac tamponade Pulmonary edema Anaphylaxis Myalgia	Assess any breathing problems, SOB, signs of pulmonary edema. Assess for peripheral edema. Monitor IV injection site for pain, swelling, and inflammation.
Alkylating Agents (Platinum analogs)	Cisplatin Carboplatin	Testicular cancer Head and neck cancer Cervix cancer Small cell lung cancer	Ototoxicity Anaphylactic-like reactions including facial edema. Renal toxicity	Monitor for tinnitus.
Plant products	Etoposide Vinblastine Vincristine	Lung cancer Testicular cancer Breast cancer Hodgkin's disease	Seizures/convulsions Liver damage-upper right side stomach pain If the WBC is severely low discontinue use of medication.	Clients may report a bad taste in the mouth. Monitor for a dry cough or wheezing. Constipation Mouth ulcers A low blood cell count may be noted. Do not give to clients with Charcot-Marie-Tooth syndrome. *Monitor for signs of an infection.
Antimetabolites	Mercaptopurine Thioguanine Fluorouracil Methotrexate	Breast Cancer Osteogenic carcinoma Acute leukemia Non-Hodgkin's lymphoma	Tablets can be taken with or without food. Mercaptopurine can also be given for Crohn's disease to reduce inflammation. Hepatotoxicity	Monitor for signs of bleeding. Tablets should be taken at the same time every day. Assess photosensitivity

Antiviral Drugs

Classification	Drug	Action	Indications	Contraindications	Side Effects	Considerations Safety
Influenza A and Respiratory Viruses Drugs	Amantadine Oseltamivir Ribavirin Rimantadine Zanamivir	Stop viral replication and the release of new influenza viruses	Acute treatment of influenza	Pregnancy and breastfeeding Renal or hepatic disease Respiratory disease (asthma, COPD)	N/V, dyspepsia, diarrhea Neuropsychiatric symptoms: delirium, delusions, hallucinations Stevens- Johnson syndrome	Pregnancy and breastfeeding Renal or hepatic disease Respiratory disease (asthma, COPD)
Herpes and Cytomegaloviruses (CMV) Drugs **Guanosine analogs**	Acyclovir Cidofovir Famciclovir Ganciclovir Valacyclovir Valganciclovir	Interfere with DNA synthesis decreases viral replication	Mucocutaneous herpes simplex virus: herpes genitalis and herpes labialis (cold sores) Varicella (chickenpox) Herpes zoster Cytomegalovirus infection	Pregnancy, breastfeeding Neurologic, renal, or hepatic disease	Headaches Agitation Confusion Myoclonus Hallucinations Encephalopathy Seizures Nausea Vomiting Diarrhea Constipation Abdominal pain **Famciclovir:** menstrual changes, hepatotoxicity Acyclovir IV use: pain or phlebitis at the injection site warnings	Stay hydrated during treatment. **Refrain from sexual activity** when sores or other signs of herpes are present. Teach the patient to always **use latex or polyurethane condoms during sex.** Take medications with plenty of water, with or without food, on a regular schedule.
Antivirals: Anti-Hepatitis agents **Nucleotide / nucleoside reverse transcriptase inhibitors (NRTIs)**	Adefovir Entecavir Tenofovir High alert meds!	Interfere with DNA synthesis and decrease viral replication	Treatment of chronic hepatitis B infection	Breastfeeding Pregnancy Children Geriatric clients Severe renal disease **Entecavir:** Impaired liver function (black box warning)	**Adefovir:** Fever, headache Gastrointestinal toxicity (nausea, abdominal pain, vomiting, diarrhea) Muscle weakness, back pain, joint pain **Tenofovir:** Nephrotoxicity	Will not completely eliminate the infection. Can transmit the virus to others. Take once each day with a full glass of water, with or without food. Infection can worsen if discontinued. Routine follow-up blood tests needed to evaluate for side effects.
Antiretrovirals: Protease Inhibitors	Indinavir Nelfinavir Atazanavir Fosamprenavir Darunavir Saquinavir Ritonavir High alert meds!	Inhibit HIV protease, preventing viral maturation.	Treatment of HIV infection in combination with other antiretrovirals	Hepatic and renal disease Diabetes Cardiac conduction disorders Hemophilia Coinfection by hepatitis B or C	Fatigue Headache Gastrointestinal side effects Hypersensitivity reactions Insulin resistance. Hyperglycemia Hyperlipidemia Hepatotoxicity Cushingoid fat redistribution Hemorrhage	**Teach patient to use latex condoms.** Take oral pills once each day with food. If miss a dose, contact healthcare provider for directions. Adhere to prescribed antiretroviral therapy. Medication does not completely eliminate virus from the body. Can transmit virus to others.

Blood Products

Drug	Whole Blood	Albumin	Plasma	Packed red Blood cells	Platelets
Route	IV	IV	IV	IV	IV
Indications	Massive transfusion Trauma Cardiovascular surgery	ARDS Cirrhotic ascites Hypovolemia Ovarian hyperstimulation syndrome Shock, Hemorrhage, Temporary replacement of albumin	Massive transfusion Severe liver disease DIC with bleeding Plasma exchange Factor deficiency with bleeding	Massive bleeding Anemia	Bleeding Severe thrombocytopenia Invasive procedures Prevention of bleeding
Side Effects	Risk for infection Immunologic reactions Volume overload Hyperkalemia Iron overload	Flushing Heart failure Hypotension Tachycardia Pruritus Skin rash Nausea Vomiting Chills, Rigors Bronchospasm Dyspnea Pulmonary edema Fever	Risk for infection, volume overload Transfusion reactions Transfusion associated circulatory overload. Transfusion related acute lung injury.	Risk for infection Immunologic reactions Volume overload Hyperkalemia Iron overload	Risk for infection, Transfusion reactions Alloimmunization and post transfusion purpura.
Contra-indications	Clients with ongoing Immunologic reactions Volume overload Hyperkalemia Iron overload	Hypersensitivity to albumin or any component of the formulation. Severe anemia Heart failure Clients with volume overload	Suspected clotting factor deficiency. Reversal of anticoagulation Bleeding of unclear etiology Unexplained abnormal clotting tests	Clients with ongoing Immunologic reactions Volume overload Hyperkalemia Iron overload	Due to the increased risk of thrombosis, the only known contraindication to platelet transfusion is thrombotic thrombocytopenic purpura (TTP).
Client Education Safety	Blood typing and crossmatching must be completed prior to transfusion.

Remain with client during the first 15 minutes.

Instruct to call if experiencing pain at infusion site, back or chest pain, chills, fever, shortness of breath, or any other concern.

Watch out for fluid volume overload. | Albumin may be given without regard to client's blood group or blood type.

Inform the client to report any irritation, swelling or wetness around the cannula site, as this may indicate that the cannula is no longer functioning correctly.

Monitor vital signs, CVP, and intake and output before and frequently. Antihistamines may be required. | Blood typing and crossmatching must be completed prior to transfusion. Volume of component for transfusion is approximately 200 ml. It is infused immediately after thawing over a 15–30-minute time frame. Remain with client during the first 15 minutes of the transfusion and obtain another set of vital signs. concern. anaphylaxis. | Blood typing and crossmatching must be completed prior to transfusion.

Volume of component for transfusion is 250–325 ml per bag, infused within 2–4 hours.

Remain with the client during the first 15 minutes of the transfusion and obtain another set of vital signs. | Blood typing and crossmatching must be completed prior to transfusion. Volume of component for transfusion ranges from 200–300 ml per bag. Platelets are infused over 15–30 minutes using the designated administration set. Assess vital signs before beginning the transfusion. Remain with client during the first 15 minutes of the transfusion and obtain another set of vital signs. Place call bell within client's reach. |

Corticosteroids

Drug	Cortisone	Prednisone	Prednisolone	Methylprednisolone	Dexamethasone	Hydrocortisone
Route	Oral, IV IM, ID Inhalation Topical, Rectal	Oral, IM IV, Topical	Oral, Topical Otic Ophthalmic	Oral, IM Intra-articular Intralesional	Oral, IM, IV Otic Ophthalmic Intra-articular Intralesional	Oral, IV Otic, Topical Rectal
Indications	Asthma and COPD Anaphylaxis Angioedema Contact dermatitis Adrenal disorders Inflammatory bowel disease Arthritis Systemic lupus erythematosus Multiple sclerosis	Anti-inflammatory Immuno-suppressive drug DermatologicGI, hematologic, eye, renal, respiratory, endocrine, or neoplastic conditions Organ transplant	Asthma Croup Nephrotic syndrome Transplant rejection Autoimmune conditions Inflammatory bowel disease Seizures Arthritis Uveitis Lymphoma Leukemia	Dermatitis, contact Erythema multiforme Stevens-Johnson syndrome Inflammatory bowel disease Autoimmune conditions Multiple sclerosis Pneumonitis Arthritis	Multiple sclerosis Cerebral edema Inflammation Shock Asthma Spinal cord compression due to metastases in oncological cases. COVID-19	Arthritis Severe allergic reactions Poison oak Dermatitis Lupus Cancer
Side Effects	Stomach upset Headache Dizziness Menstrual changes Trouble sleeping Increased appetite Weight gain	Skin fragility Weight gain Increased risk of infections Fractures. Hypertension Hyperglycemia Dyslipidemia	Nausea Heartburn Headache Dizziness Menstrual period changes Trouble sleeping Increased sweating Acne	Dizziness Insomnia Depression Anxiety Acne Hirsutism Bruising Metrorrhagia Skin rash Edema Vision change Infections Weak muscles Black stool	GI upset Headache Dizziness Insomnia Depression Anxiety Acne Easy bruising Metrorrhagia Edema Vision change Infections Weak muscles Black stools	Burning Itching Irritation Redness, or dryness of the skin Acne Unwanted hair growth Severe rash Redness
Contra-indications	Allergic reaction Live-attenuated vaccines Systemic infection Osteoporosis Glaucoma Hypertension Herpes simplex Keratitis Varicella infections Peptic ulcers CHF	Allergic reaction Systemic fungal infections Live-attenuated vaccines	Allergic reaction Systemic fungal infections	Allergic reactions Systemic fungal infection Live virus vaccine Thrombo-cytopenic purpura, Peptic ulcers Heart disease Diabetes Osteoporosis Glaucoma	Systemic fungal infections Live vaccines Cirrhosis Diverticulitis Myasthenia gravis Renal disease Peptic ulcers Ulcerative colitis	Allergic reactions Live attenuated vaccines Systemic fungal infection Osteoporosis Diabetes mellitus Glaucoma Peptic ulcer disease.
Client Education Safety	Infection/illness is a greater risk. Blood glucose may increase. Corticosteroids may cause dizziness.	Vision changes may occur. Monitor blood glucose. Levels. Do not abruptly stop taking.	Mental changes may occur. Mood swings may occur.	Bone density and blood sugar should be monitored. Children's growth and development should be monitored.	Take with meals or milk. Increased cancer risk	Aspirin, and ibuprofen may interact with hydrocortisone. Monitor skin irritation.

Study more at ReMarNurse.com | Join live weekly on YouTube @ReMarNurse

Diuretics

Drug	Carbonic Anhydrase Inhibitors	Loop Diuretics	Osmotic Diuretics	Potassium Sparing	Thiazide
Route	Oral	Oral or IV	IV	Orally or IV	Oral
Indications	Treating glaucoma. Also, can be used as adjunctive therapy for epilepsy, edema and some metabolic disorders	Edema is caused by conditions like CHF, liver cirrhosis or kidney dysfunction. May be used to lower high blood pressure.	Acute renal failure to increase urine output. Reduction of ICP, in conditions such as cerebral edema, traumatic brain injury, Reduces intraocular pressure.	Hypertension Edema: In conditions such as heart failure, liver cirrhosis or kidney disease. Hyperaldosteronism	Hypertension: treatment Can be used to treat edema. Nephrolithiasis:
Side Effects	Frequent urination, increased thirst, drowsiness, loss of appetite. Tingling or numbness in the extremities, skin rash, kidney stones and metabolic acidosis.	Electrolyte imbalances: excessive loss of K+, Na and Mg. Dehydration, dizziness: Ototoxicity Allergic reactions	Electrolyte imbalances: excessive loss of K+, Na, and Mg. Prolonged or excessive use of osmotic diuretics can potentially result in renal impairment.	Regular monitoring of K+ levels is essential as levels increase. Gynecomastia (in males) May also cause menstrual irregularities in women.	Can cause low K+ in the blood. Hyperuricemia: increase the level of gout attacks. Hyperglycemia Electrolyte imbalances: Erectile dysfunction
Contra-indications	Severe kidney, or liver dysfunction. Adrenal gland failure and electrolyte imbalances such as hypokalemia. Avoid a history of allergic reactions.	Anuria Dehydration Gout Severe electrolyte imbalances: Na, K+, or Mg in the blood, should not be described as they may worsen fluid depletion.	Anuria, or Severe Heart Failure Active Intracranial Bleeding: as they can worsen bleeding by increasing intracranial pressure. Severe dehydration	Severe kidney dysfunction Hyperkalemia Concomitant use of ACE Inhibitors, vancomycin, or other nephrotoxic medications.	Severe Kidney Dysfunction- may be less effective. If hypersensitivity then avoid using them. Thiazide diuretics may be less
Client Education **Safety**	Maintain Hydration. May cause dizziness. Avoid consuming alcohol. Monitor K+ and kidney function.	Maintain adequate fluid intake. Electrolyte Balance: Position changes: To prevent dizziness or orthostatic hypotension, clients should be cautious when changing positions. Eat foods high in potassium.	Dose adjustments and treatment duration will be determined by MD. May cause congestive heart failure or pulmonary edema. May be prescribed for dialysis disequilibrium syndrome.	Dietary: Avoid excessive consumption of high-potassium foods, such as bananas, oranges, tomatoes and spinach. Clients should know the signs of hyperkalemia, such as muscle weakness, irregular heartbeat, or tingling sensations, and report them.	Ensure proper intake of potassium-rich foods. Fluid Intake: Thiazide diuretics increase urine production, so clients should drink an adequate amount of fluids to prevent dehydration. NSAIDS decrease effectiveness. Allergy to sulfa medications.

Erectile Dysfunction

Drug	Sildenafil	Tadalafil	Vardenafil	Avanafil
Route	Oral	Oral	Oral	Oral
Indications	Erectile dysfunction (ED) Pulmonary arterial hypertension (PAH) in both men and women.	Erectile dysfunction (ED) Enlarged prostate (benign prostatic hyperplasia)	Erectile dysfunction (ED) in adult men. It helps increase blood flow to the penis.	Erectile dysfunction (ED) in adult men. It helps increase blood flow to the penis.
Side Effects	Headache Nose bleeds Flushing Indigestion Diarrhea Nasal congestion Dizziness Visual changes	Headache Flushing Indigestion Back pain Muscle aches Nasal congestion Dizziness Serious side effects are rare but may include sudden vision or hearing loss, chest pain, or an allergic reaction.	Upset stomach Facial flushing Indigestion Nasal congestion Back pain Muscle aches lightheadedness	Flushing in the upper body. Indigestion Nasal congestion Back pain Muscle aches Dizziness Serious side effects, although rare, may include vision or hearing changes.
Contra-indications	Do not take with nitrates or nitric oxide donors (e.g., nitroglycerin), as it can result in severe hypotension. Do not take with certain medications (e.g., alpha-blockers) With certain eye conditions (e.g. non-arteritic anterior ischemic optic neuropathy) Do not give with grapefruit juice.	Do not give with severe liver or kidney disease. Receiving treatment with certain medications used for the treatment of pulmonary arterial hypertension (PAH) Avoid grapefruit juice.	Do not take with nitrates or nitric oxide donors (e.g., nitroglycerin), as it can cause a significant drop in blood pressure. It can be taken with or without food, but a high-fat meal may reduce its effectiveness. Do not consume grapefruit or grapefruit juice while taking.	Do not take grapefruit juice. Do not take with nitrates as low blood pressure could occur.
Client Education **Safety**	Take 30 minutes before activity. Do not take with a high fat meal. Do not take this with grapefruit juice. This medication will not prevent sexually transmitted diseases.	This can be taken with or without food. Take at least 30 minutes before sexual activity. Does not offer protection against sexual transmitted diseases. Call doctor if prolonged erection occurs longer than 4 hours.	Do not take more than once a day and never take more than the prescribed dose. Do not take with alpha blockers or nitrates. Report chest pain immediately or prolonged erection longer than 4 hours.	It can be taken with or without food, but a high-fat meal may reduce its effectiveness. Does not protect against sexually transmitted infections. Notify the MD if priapism as it can lead to permanent damage to the penis.

GERD/GI Medications

Drug	Magnesium Hydroxide Salts	Antacids	Histamine 2 Blockers	Proton pump inhibitor	Simethicone	Sucralfate	Loperamide
Route	Oral	Oral	Oral, IV or IM	Oral or IV	Oral	Oral, Rectal or Topical	Oral
Indications	Dyspepsia Heartburn GERD Constipation	Acid reflux Heartburn Stomach lining Stress Stomach ulcers	Heartburn GERD Peptic ulcers Upper GI bleeding Zollinger-Ellison syndrome	Acid reflux GERD Ulcers Esophagitis Zollinger-Ellison Syndrome H. pylori infections	Flatulence Bloating Helicobacter pylori	Dyspepsia Duodenal ulcers Chemo-therapy-induced mucositis. Ulcers	Acute nonspecific diarrhea
Side Effects	Diarrhea Constipation Loss of appetite Unusual tiredness Muscle weakness	Constipation Headache N/V Stomach cramps *Serious side effects Acid rebound Neuro-toxicity anemia Osteopenia High serum Ca + levels	Headaches Drowsiness Muscle pain Breast swelling Confusion Congestion Rash Drowsiness Irritability Anxiety N/V Diarrhea Fever	Headache Diarrhea Constipation Nausea Infections Bone fractures Increased risk of Clostridium difficile Osteo-porosis Low vitamin B12 levels	Nausea Constipation Diarrhea Headache *Serious side effects may include Dizziness Fainting Slow/irregular heartbeat and breathing Mental/mood changes	Constipation Hives Rash Itching Difficulty breathing or swallowing. Swelling of the face, throat, tongue, or lips	Dry mouth, Drowsiness, Abdominal discomfort Allergic reaction
Contra-indications	Pregnant Breast-feeding Renal failure Magnesium restricted diet Appendicitis Myocardial infarction or heart block. Fecal impaction	Allergic reactions Renal failure Heart failure Edema, Cirrhosis Low-Na diets Uremia GI-hemorrhages Renal calculus Achlorhydria	Allergic reactions Pregnancy Breast-feeding Hepatic and Nephrotic dysfunction May affect vitamin B 12 absorption.	Allergic reactions Pregnancy Severe hepatic disease Decreases the effectiveness of blood thinners. Avoid if Mg levels are low in the blood.	Allergic reactions Can decrease thyroid medication effectiveness. Can cause false negative guaiac stool test	Allergic reaction End-stage renal disease Uncontrolled Diabetes mellitus Impaired swallowing /gag reflex	Do not give to children less than 2 years of age. Do give with tonic water or grapefruit juice. Do not give with anti-depressants can cause cardiac arrest.
Client Education Safety	Do not take any medications within 2 hours of taking an antacid. Reacts with digoxin, and cimetidine.	May contain aspirin.	Confusion and dizziness are more likely to develop in elderly clients. Do not mix with Warfarin	Take 30 minutes before a meal.	Induce low phosphate levels. Simethicone liquid drops can be given to infants.	High blood sugar may occur if sucralfate is used in diabetic. Do not consume antacids within 30 minutes of taking sucralfate.	Avoid alcohol. Avoid tasks that require mental alertness. Teach client to report if diarrhea does not stop within 3 days, Assess bowel sounds for peristalsis.

Herbal Medications

Drug	Ginkgo biloba	Ginseng	Ginger	Saw palmetto	Black cohosh	St. John's wort	Kava Kava	Echinacea
Route	Oral	Oral	Oral	Oral	Oral	Oral Topical	Oral	Oral Topical
Indications	Anxiety Alzheimer disease Hearing loss Mental illness Tardive dyskinesia Dementia	Control Hyper-glycemia High cholesterol Improve energy level	Motion sickness High BP Nausea Bloating digestion. Pain relief Prevent cardio-vascular disease	Improve surgery outcomes of TURP. Improves urine flow Reduces nighttime urination. Prevent androgenic alopecia	Meno-pausal symptoms Hot flashes Menstrual cramps Muscle and joint pain. Promote liver and nervous system function.	Depression Mood disorder Menopausal symptoms Emotional distress Somatic symptom disorder	Anxiety including generalized anxiety disorder Stress Insomnia PMS	Coughs and colds Bronchitis Upper respiratory infections Gingivitis Canker sores Yeast infections
Side Effects	Stomach upset Headache Dizziness Allergic skin reactions. Bruising and bleeding Arrhythmias	Headache Insomnia Nausea Diarrhea Tachy-cardia Bleeding Breast pain Menstrual problems	Irritation of the mouth Diarrhea Heartburn Bleeding	Diarrhea Headache Fatigue Decreased libido Nausea Vomiting Vertigo	GI Upset Cramping Headache Rash Vaginal bleeding Weight gain Dizziness	Diarrhea Dizziness Trouble sleeping Restlessness Skin tingling.	Dyspnea Visual changes, Photo-phobia Changes to platelets, RBCs and WBCs Liver damage Dermatitis	Nausea Stomach pain Rashes
Contra-indications	Bronchial asthma Allergic reactions Hypotension Seizure Pregnancy Breast-feeding Diabetics	Pregnancy Insomnia Bleeding disorders Estrogen conditions HTN Auto-immune disorder	Children under 2 Heartburn Mouth irritation Surgery Bleeding disorders Cholelithiasis	Pregnancy Breast-feeding Hormone related cancer Surgery	History of Breast cancer Blood clotting disorders Hypertension Endo-metriosis Fibroids	Pregnancy Attention Deficit Disorder Schizophrenia Alzheimer's Disease Bipolar disorder	Children Pregnant Breast-feeding Liver or Kidney disorders	Asthma Cancer Auto-immune disorders Organ transplant Diabetes Alcohol dependence Liver disease.
Client Education **Safety**	Eating Fresh SEEDS can result in death. Interacts with blood thinners like aspirin. Do not take with SSRI. Do not take with MAOIs.	Do not take with blood thinners. Can cause tachy-cardia with caffeine. Increases effective-ness of anti-diabetics .	Do not exceed 4 grams a day. Increases risk of bleeding. May reduce blood glucose levels.	Stop taking 2 weeks before surgery. May reduce the effects of oral contraceptives.	May cause liver damage, urine may change dark. Change positions slowly.	Photo-sensitivity may occur. Avoid direct sunlight. Do not take with SSRI or MAOIs as interactions can occur.	Kava prolongs the effect of anesthesia. Do not take with alcohol. May increase effects of benzodiazepines.	Increases the effect of caffeine and alcohol. May interfere with corti-costeroid use.

Hormonal Contraceptives

Classification	Oral Contraceptives	Vaginal rings	Patch	Implants	Intramuscular injections
Generic Names	Combination tablets (estrogen and progestin) Progestin-only tablets	Two types of rings are available: -One that should be replaced every month. -One that should be yearly replaced.	Ethinyl Estradiol; Norelgestromin Patches	Etonogestrel Implant	Medroxyprogesterone acetate
Indications	Continuous contraception Menstrual cramps Premenstrual syndrome Iron deficiency anemia Noncancerous (benign) breast disorders Ovarian cysts Cancer of the uterus and ovaries	A vaginal ring is a tiny, flexible ring inserted inside the vagina to prevent pregnancy. It's worn for three weeks and then removed for one week.	ETHINYL ESTRADIOL; NORELGESTROMIN is a patch that prevents ovulation. This combination of estrogen and progestin is attached to the skin. A patch that attaches to the skin.	Etonogestrel is an implant that also prevents ovulation. The implant is inserted by a healthcare provider under the skin of the upper arm. It contains a progestin hormone.	The shot works by preventing ovulation and thickening the cervical mucus preventing sperm from successfully traveling to the egg. This is injected intramuscularly and is given every 12 weeks or three months.
Side effects	Breakthrough bleeding Nausea Bloating Fluid retention Breast tenderness headaches Acne, change in mood and appetite. Blood clots. Higher risk of developing cervical cancer.	A regular menstrual period is expected. Breakthrough bleeding is uncommon. Side effects are similar to those who take combination oral contraceptives.	ALLERGIC REACTION Chest pain Fluid retention abdominal pain, nausea, and vomiting Fever, Hypertension Loss of appetite light-colored stool dark yellow or brown urine, jaundice Fatigue, Unusual vaginal discharge Mood swings Breast tenderness Melasma Irregular menstrual cycles, Weight gain	ALLERGIC REACTION Chest pain Nausea/vomiting Fever Hypertension Dark yellow or brown urine Jaundice Fatigue Headache Slurred speech Confusion Mood swings Breast tenderness Melasma Irregular menstrual cycles Weight gain	Irregular menstruation to no period at all. Headaches. Nervousness. Depression. Acne. Changes in appetite. Weight gain. Excessive facial or body hair Hair loss. Osteoporosis.
Considerations Safety	Take regularly once a day for 21 to 24 days, then skipped for 4 to 7 days where menstrual period will occur, If client forgets to take a pill, two tablets should be taken the next day. Diabetics should use in caution.	Should be used for three weeks and rest for a week for menstruation to occur. Use for the first 5 days of menstruation or as a backup method for the next 7 days to prevent pregnancy. The woman herself can place them. The ring is usually not felt during intercourse.	The area should be clean, dry, and healthy. Press the patch firmly for ten seconds. Changing the patch every 7 days on the same day for three weeks is important. Rest for seven days, then apply a new patch after. Hypersensitivity to sunlight may also occur. If undergoing surgery or MRI, it is advised to stop using this contraceptive.	An implant is inserted under the skin on the inner part of the upper arm by a trained healthcare provider. A user card is given once the implant is inserted. The location of the implant and when to remove it are indicated on the card.	Shots are given every three months. The first dose is given within the first week of the onset of menstruation. Client must receive another shot once every 12 weeks to be fully protected. Immediate protection after the first dose of injection if it is during the menstrual period. If it is given after menstruation then wait 10 days before having intercourse without using other contraceptives to prevent pregnancy.

Insulins

Drug	Insulin Aspart	Insulin Lispro	Regular insulin	Intermediate Insulin	Insulin Detemir	Insulin glargine	Humulin 70/30
Route	Subcutaneous	Subcutaneous	Subcutaneous IV	Subcutaneous	Subcutaneous	Subcutaneous	Subcutaneous
Indication	To manage blood sugar levels.	To manage blood sugar levels.	To manage blood sugar levels.	To manage blood sugar levels.	To manage blood sugar levels.	To manage blood sugar levels.	To manage blood sugar levels.
Side Effects	Hypoglycemia Hypokalemia Injection site reactions Allergic reactions	Hypoglycemia Hypokalemia Injection site reactions Allergic reactions	Hypoglycemia Weight gain	Hypoglycemia Hypokalemia Injection site reactions Allergic reactions	Hypo-glycemia Hypokalemia Injection site reactions Allergic reactions	Hypo-glycemia Hypokalemia Injection site reactions Allergic reactions	Hypo-glycemia Hypokalemia Injection site reactions Allergic reactions
Contra-indications	Hypoglycemia Allergy Diabetic Ketoacidosis	Hypoglycemia Allergy Diabetic Ketoacidosis	Hypoglycemia Allergy	Hypoglycemia Allergy Diabetic Ketoacidosis	Hypo-glycemia Allergy Diabetic Ketoacidosis Low potassium levels Do not give with furosemide.	Hypo-glycemia Allergy Diabetic Ketoacidosis Not for patients younger than 6 years old.	Hypo-glycemia Allergy Diabetic Ketoacidosis
Client Education **Safety**	Administer with meals. Do not mix with any other insulin. Onset 15 minutes Peak 1-2 hrs. Duration 3-6 hrs. May cause hypokalemia	Administer with meals. Do not mix with any other insulin. Onset 15 minutes Peak 1-2 hrs. Duration 3-6 hrs. May cause hypokalemia.	Only use insulin needles when giving SQ. Regular insulin can be added to hemodialysis. Onset 30-60 minutes Peak 2-4 hours Duration 6-10 hours	Intermediate insulin is cloudy in appearance. Use a new needle with every injection. Inject insulin at the same time each day. Onset 1-2 hrs. Peak 2-4 hrs. Duration >12 hrs.	Never share needles can result in blood borne infections. Do not use if the liquid is thick or cloudy. It should appear clear. May cause lipodystrophy May cause weight gain. Do not take with aspirin as will increase the effects. Onset 1-2 hours Peak 12-24 hours Duration Varies	Do not give to patients who have hypoglycemia. Sulfamethoxazole Trimethoprim increases the risk of hypoglycemia when taken with the medication. Lowers blood sugar over 24 hours. Rotate injection sites and never inject into the muscle. Onset 1-2 hours Peak NO Peak Duration 24 hours	70% is intermediate 30% is regular insulin. Rotate injection sites Beta blockers, clonidine, and lithium salts will increase effectiveness of the insulin. Onset 30-60 minutes Peak 2-10 hrs. Duration 10-18 hours.

 Study more at ReMarNurse.com | Join live weekly on YouTube @ReMarNurse

Labor & Delivery

Drug	Oxytocin	Terbutaline Sulfate	Ritodrine	Butorphanol	Magnesium sulfate	Methergine
Route	IM, IV, Topical	Oral, IM, SC Inhalation	Oral, IV	IV, IM, Nasal	Oral, IM, IV Intraosseous	Oral, IM, IV
Indications	Improve uterine contractions. To deliver the placenta Postpartum hemorrhage To promote lactation	To stop or slow uterine contractions. To treat wheezing and shortness of breath caused by lung conditions	Premature labor	Pain relief It can be administered before childbirth, surgery, or general anesthesia.	A tocolytic used to suppress preterm labor. Magnesium lowers the Ca+ in the uterine muscles which relaxes the muscles.	Routine management of uterine atony, hemorrhage, and subinvolution of the uterus.
Side Effects	Arrhythmias Permanent CNS damage Neonatal seizure Fetal death Uteroplacental hypoperfusion Maternal Hypotension	Nervousness Dizziness Headache Hypertension ***Serious side effects including: Tachycardia Chest pain Muscle cramps Weakness Seizures.	Blurred vision Chest pain Dizziness Dry mouth Flushed skin Fruit-like breath odor Increased urination Loss of appetite Nausea	Coughing Dyspnea Chest tightness Wheezing Blurred vision Confusion Lightheadedness Bloody nose Body aches Nasal irritation	Diarrhea Shock Respiratory paralysis Hypothermia Pulmonary edema Hypotension Hypocalcemia Hypo-phosphatemia Hyperkalemia Cold feeling	Allergic reactions Ototoxicity Increased BP Chest pain Paresthesia Seizures Headaches Sudden numbness or weakness
Contra-indications	Hyper-sensitivity Fetal distress Hydramnios Placenta previa Prematurity Uterine rupture. Carcinoma, Active herpes genitalis.	Hypersensitivity Prolonged Tocolysis	Antepartum hemorrhage Eclampsia Intrauterine fetal death Cardiac disease Threatened miscarriage. Placenta previa Cord compression	Significant respiratory depression Acute or severe bronchial asthma. Pregnancy Breastfeeding	Hypersensitivity reaction Heart block Preeclampsia eclampsia- two hours before fetal delivery. Kidney disease-	Hypertension Toxemia Pregnancy Hypersensitivity.
Client Education Safety	If uterine hyperactivity discontinues *Monitor for symptoms of water intoxication. Record I & O Monitor the fetal HR/maternal BP and pulse at least every 15 minutes Oxytocin may be transmitted in milk.	Report hypersensitivity reactions or worsening bronchospasm This drug may cause dizziness. Avoid use of Alcohol or marijuana Do not drive, use machinery, or do anything that needs alertness until safe.	Report immediately if the contractions start again Ritodrine may cause hypovolemia and may affect blood pressure. Monitoring of client's vital signs, electrolytes and cardiac function is required.	Increase the effects of alcohol and other CNS depressants. Encourage them to refrain from operating machinery, driving, etc. due to the effects of butorphanol, which include drowsiness, confusion, and disorientation.	May cause fetal abnormalities if used longer than 5-7 days. May cause reduced respiratory rate, muscle weakness, and hypotension. May reduce respirations. Calcium gluconate is the antidote.	Breast-feeding should be avoided throughout methergine treatment and for at least 12 hours after the last dosage. Methergine should not be given intravenously regularly as it can cause a hypertensive crisis.

Laxatives

Drug	Bulk forming laxatives	Stimulants laxatives	Osmotic laxatives	Stool softeners	Polystyrene sulfonate
Route	Oral	Oral & Rectal	Oral & Rectal	Oral	Oral & Rectal
Indications	Constipation Fecal impaction Mild chronic Diarrhea	Constipation Fecal impaction	Constipation Fecal impaction. Bowel preparation prior to surgery Hepatic encephalopathy	Constipation	Hyperkalemia Hepatic encephalopathy
Side Effects	Abdominal distention Flatulence	Abdominal pain or cramping may occur with stimulant laxative use.	Flatulence, abdominal cramps Nausea are common. Phosphate enemas	Stomach pain Abdominal cramps Nausea, Diarrhea May cause urine discoloration	High dosages can cause anorexia, nausea, vomiting, sodium retention, Peripheral edema Increased weight
Contra-indications	Intestinal obstruction Fecal impaction Ileus Do not routinely use bulk-forming laxatives with new-onset constipation who have recently had abdominal surgery	Stimulant laxatives should not be used in clients with intestinal obstruction as this could induce perforation. Rectal preparations are usually avoided if hemorrhoids or an anal fissure is present.	Osmotic laxatives are contraindicated in intestinal obstruction as there is a risk of perforation. Phosphate enemas can cause significant fluid shifts so they should be used with caution in heart failure, ascites and when electrolyte disturbances are present.	Intestinal obstruction, symptoms of appendicitis, acute abdominal pain, and fecal impaction, especially in children.	Clients with low potassium levels, neonates with reduced GI motility, intestinal obstruction, perforation, any postoperative client until normal bowel function resumes.
Client Education **Safety**	Explain the laxative works as a fiber supplement. Advise client to take the laxative with a meal and plenty of fluid. Monitor treatment response with a stool chart.	Encourage good oral fluid intake as this will help in passage of stools. Aim for 6–8 glasses of liquid per day. Advise your client that stimulant laxatives do not work immediately	Clients should have at least 6–8 glasses of liquid per day. Osmotic laxatives may be taken with or without food. When treating fecal impaction with rectally administered laxatives, try a glycerol suppository before using a phosphate enema. Glycerol suppositories are less likely to cause electrolyte disturbance.	Educate clients on effective measures to promote defecation such as increasing fluid intake, exercise, high-fiber diet. Discourage client using longer than 1 week. May give each dose with a full glass of water or fruit juice. Assess bowel sounds for peristalsis. Record time of evacuation.	Let the client know that the effectiveness of the medication may take a few hours to days. Monitor serum potassium levels regularly. Also monitor serum magnesium, and calcium levels. Monitor daily pattern of bowel activity, stool consistency.

Osteoporosis Medications

Drug	Alendronate	Ibandronate	Risedronate	Zoledronic Acid
Route	Oral	Oral, IV	Oral	IV
Indications	Osteoporosis Paget's disease Osteopenia associated with cystic fibrosis Osteopenia, Osteopenia with rheumatology issues.	Osteoporosis Postmenopausal osteoporosis prevention Metastatic bone disease Hypercalcemia Bone pain	Osteoporosis in postmenopausal women. Paget's disease of bone (osteitis deformans). Treatment and prevention of postmenopausal, glucocorticoid-induced osteoporosis and osteoporosis in men.	Osteoporosis Paget's disease Bone metastases Multiple myeloma Hypercalcemia of malignancy Postmenopausal women with breast cancer
Side Effects	Back pain abdominal pain Nausea Constipation, diarrhea, and flatulence. Over dosage can cause hypocalcemia, hypophosphatemia, and other significant GI disturbances.	Atypical femur fractures GI mucosal irritation Hypocalcemia Influenza like illness Osteonecrosis of the jaw Abdominal pain, dyspepsia, constipation, nausea, diarrhea.	Arthralgia. Rash, diarrhea, constipation, nausea, abdominal pain, dyspepsia, flu like symptoms, peripheral edema, bone pain, sinusitis, asthenia, dry eye, tinnitus. Overdose produces hypocalcemia	Fever, nausea, vomiting, constipation, hypotension, anxiety, insomnia, flu-like symptoms. Acute kidney injury, atrial fibrillation Atypical femur fractures, hypocalcemia, influenza like illness and osteonecrosis of the jaw.
Contra-indications	Allergic reactions Hypocalcemia abnormalities of the esophagus, Clients with inability to stand or sit upright for at least 30 minutes. It is also not recommended in clients with renal insufficiency.	Allergic reactions abnormalities of the esophagus that would delay emptying, hypocalcemia. Precaution in clients with GI diseases (duodenitis, dysphagia, esophagitis, gastritis, ulcers, renal impairment with creatinine clearance less than 30 ml/min.	Allergic reactions bisphosphonates (e.g., etidronate, tiludronate, alendronate); hypocalcemia; inability to stand or sit upright for at least 30 min; abnormalities of the esophagus. Precaution with clients having bone, surgery, and renal impairment.	Allergic reactions renal impairment, bone fractures, history of aspirin-sensitive asthma, clients with disturbances of calcium and mineral metabolism (e.g., hypoparathyroidism, malabsorption syndrome)
Client Education Safety	Must be taken with 6–8 oz) of plain water, first thing in the morning and at least 30 min prior to eating or drinking. Other beverages significantly reduce absorption of medication. Supplemental calcium and vitamin D should be taken if dietary intake inadequate. To avoid esophageal irritation do not lie down for at least 30 min after taking medication.	Hypocalcemia, vitamin D deficiency must be corrected before beginning therapy. Must be taken with 6–8 oz) of plain water, first thing in the morning and at least 30 min prior to eating or drinking. Other beverages significantly reduce absorption of medication. To avoid esophageal irritation do not lie down for at least 30 min after taking medication.	Teach client to report swallowing difficulties, chest pain, Assess symptoms of Paget's disease. Hypocalcemia, vitamin D deficiency must be corrected before therapy begins. Must be taken with 6–8 oz) of plain water, first thing in the morning and at least 30 min prior to eating or drinking. To avoid esophageal irritation do not lie down for at least 30 min after taking medication.	Dental clearance for clients is warranted prior to starting treatment due to risk for osteonecrosis. Assess vertebral bone mass, renal and liver function prior to starting treatment. Hypocalcemia, vitamin D deficiency must be corrected before beginning therapy. Obtain laboratory baselines such as serum chemistries, renal function. Obtain results of bone density study.

Proton Pump Inhibitors

Drug	Lansoprazole	Omeprazole	Pantoprazole	Rabeprazole	Esomeprazole
Route	Oral	Oral or IV	Oral or IV	Oral	Oral or IV
Indications	GERD Peptic ulcers Zollinger-Ellison Syndrome H. pylori activity	Gastroesophageal Reflux Disease Peptic ulcers Zollinger-Ellison Syndrome H. pylori activity	Gastroesophageal Reflux Disease Peptic ulcers Zollinger-Ellison Syndrome H. pylori activity	Gastroesophageal Reflux Disease Peptic ulcers Zollinger-Ellison Syndrome H. pylori activity	Gastroesophageal Reflux Disease Peptic ulcers Zollinger-Ellison Syndrome H. pylori activity
Side Effects	Headache, N/V Diarrhea Constipation Dizziness or drowsiness Rash Bone fractures	Fatigue Mouth ulcers Leg pain Constipation Frequent need to urinate Rash Bone fractures	Headache Diarrhea Bone fractures Abdominal pain or discomfort Gas or bloating Hypertension Changes in taste sensation	Headache Diarrhea or constipation Nausea or vomiting Abdominal pain Sore throat	Headache Nausea Diarrhea Abdominal pain Constipation
Contra-indications	Avoid if clients have liver or kidney dysfunction. Do not give if client is taking ampicillin.	Do not give if the client has liver or kidney dysfunction. Do not give with clopidogrel, methotrexate, or St. John's wort. Avoid all blood thinners with this medication.	Allergic reactions may occur. Do not take with medications containing rilpivirine. May cause osteoporosis with long term use.	Allergic reactions can occur. Do not give if clients have liver or kidney dysfunction.	Do not give if the patient has liver or kidney damage. Children are more susceptible to respiratory infections while taking this medication.
Client Education **Safety**	Allergic reactions may occur. Bronchospasm may occur. May interfere with HIV medication. Can be given with other antibiotics to treat H. pylori.	May cause osteoporosis with long term use. Severe diarrhea may occur. Mouth ulcers may occur.	Withdrawal: Abruptly stopping pantoprazole after prolonged use may lead to rebound hyperacidity. May cause low magnesium in the blood.	Allergic reactions can occur. May cause mouth ulcers. May decrease the effectiveness of blood thinners.	Allergic reactions will occur. Watch for bronchospasm. Increases risk for bone fractures.

Nursing School is temporary but being a nurse is a LIFETIME calling!

Respiratory Medications

Drug	Theophylline	Albuterol	Montelukast	Fluticasone propionate
Route	Oral, IV	Inhalation	Oral	Inhalation, Nasal, Topical
Indications	Chronic Obstructive Pulmonary Disease Asthma Infant Apnea Anosmia Chronic Bronchitis	Asthma Bronchospasm	Asthma Exercise-Induced Bronchoconstriction (EIB) Seasonal Allergic Rhinitis	Asthma Inflammatory and Pruritic dermatoses Allergic and nonallergic rhinitis.
Side Effects	Upset stomach Stomach pain Loose bowel movement Headache Restlessness Difficulty falling asleep or staying asleep Irritability Vomiting Tachycardia Arrhythmia seizures Rashes	Uncontrollable shaking of a part of the body Nervousness Headache Nausea Vomiting Cough Throat irritation Muscle, bone, or back pain Tachycardia Arrhythmia Allergic reaction Dysphagia Hoarseness	Upper respiratory infection Fever Headache Sore throat Cough Stomach pain Diarrhea Earache or ear infection Flu Runny nose Sinus infection.	Bloody nose Chest tightness Cough Headache Muscle aches Facial tenderness Sore throat White patches in the mouth and throat Earache Fever Lower abdominal or stomach pain Nausea Pain on passing urine
Contra-indications	Hypersensitivity reaction to xanthine derivatives Coronary artery disease Cystic Fibrosis Hepatic impairment Hyperthyroidism Peptic ulcer disease Seizure disorders	Allergy to milk proteins Diabetes Heart disease QT prolongation Hypertension Hyperthyroidism Hypokalemia Ketoacidosis Seizures Kidney disease	Hypersensitivity Phenylketonuria (PKU)	Hypersensitivity Status asthmaticus Acute episode of asthma Acute COPD
Client Education Safety	Caffeine-rich beverages and foods like coffee, tea, cocoa, and chocolate can worsen theophylline's adverse effects. The nurse should monitor the following in the client receiving Theophylline because of its narrow therapeutic window and many side effects, Heart rate Headache Insomnia Irritability Respiratory rate	Albuterol may cause hypokalemia Decreased urine Dry mouth Polydipsia Arrhythmia Loss of appetite Mood changes Myalgia Nausea Vomiting Numbness or tingling in the hands, feet, or lips Dyspnea Seizures Fatigue	The use of montelukast sodium has been linked to neuropsychiatric problems such as agitation, aggressive behavior, anxiety, and suicidal thoughts. Montelukast is not given to treat sudden attack of asthma symptoms. If the patient needs a prescription for a short-acting inhaler to use during attacks, they should consult with their doctor.	Fluticasone may cause holes or ulcers in the cartilage of the nose and delay wound healing. The client should inform the doctor if they had nose surgery, a nose injury, or a nose infection in the last few months before using this medicine. Fluticasone may cause serious allergic reactions, including anaphylaxis. Candida or yeast infection may occur.

Skeletal Muscle Relaxants

Drug	Baclofen	Carisoprodol	Chlorzoxazone	Cyclobenzaprine	Dantrolene
Route	Oral, Intrathecal	Oral	Oral	Oral	Oral, Intravenous
Indications	Spasticity muscle stiffness, Rigidity Cerebral palsy, or spinal cord injury	Musculoskeletal pain Muscle spasms, sprains, strains, or injuries	Acute musculoskeletal pain muscle spasms, sprains, strains, or injuries.	Cyclobenzapine is used for the relief of muscle spasms and associated pain or discomfort caused by musculoskeletal conditions, such as sprains, strains, or injuries.	Dantrolene is primarily used to treat muscle spasms and spasticity associated with conditions like cerebral palsy, multiple sclerosis, spinal cord injury, stroke, and neuroleptic malignant syndrome.
Side Effects	Drowsiness Muscle weakness Nausea or vomiting Headache Insomnia Constipation or diarrhea Urinary retention Dry mouth Gait changes	Drowsiness, Headache Upset stomach Flushing Dry mouth Allergic reactions	Drowsiness Upset stomach Headache Skin rash or hypersensitivity reactions (rare)	Drowsiness Dry mouth Dizziness Fatigue or weakness Blurred vision Constipation Urinary retention	Sedation Weakness or fatigue Dizziness Diarrhea or constipation Nausea or vomiting Urinary frequency or incontinence - Liver toxicity (rare but serious)
Contra-indications	Known hypersensitivity A history of hypersensitivity or an allergic reaction to GABA-B Severe paralysis. - Active peptic ulcer disease	Hypersensitivity Acute intermittent porphyria A history of substance abuse or dependence Severe renal or hepatic impairment.	Hypersensitivity to chlorzoxazone Hepatic impairment	Hypersensitivity Acute recovery phase of myocardial infarction. Heart conduction disorders or arrhythmias. Concurrent or use of monoamine oxidase inhibitors (MAOIs).	Hypersensitivity Active liver disease A genetic condition called malignant hyperthermia.
Client Education Safety	Can cause drowsiness and impair coordination. Avoid consuming alcohol. Regularly monitor blood pressure, liver function, and renal function as directed.	Avoid driving or operating heavy machinery. Avoid consuming alcohol. Report any allergic reactions. Do not stop taking abruptly. This medication can become addictive.	Avoid driving or operating. Avoid consuming alcohol. Report any allergic reactions, severe dizziness, or difficulty breathing. Monitor liver function.	Avoid activities that require alertness. Report any adverse effects, such as difficulty breathing, chest pain. Take measures to prevent constipation.	May cause drowsiness. Avoid alcohol consumption. Can cause liver toxicity. Watch for mental changes and hallucinations.

Sympathomimetics

Drug	Epinephrine	Norepinephrine	Phenylephrine	Dopamine
Route	IM, IV, Subcutaneous, Inhalation	Intravenous	Oral tablets Nasal sprays Eye drops Injectables	Intravenous
Indications	Emergency situations to treat severe allergic reactions, also known as anaphylaxis. Cardiac arrest situations Asthma attacks	Critically low blood pressure Septic shock, Cardiogenic shock It helps increase blood pressure.	Nasal congestion relief due to allergies or colds Pupil dilation during eye examinations Short-term increase in blood pressure	Low blood pressure (hypotension) that may result from conditions like septic shock, cardiogenic shock, or low blood volume. Heart failure with low cardiac output
Side Effects	Increased heart rate Increased blood pressure Palpitations Anxiety or nervousness Headache Dizziness or lightheadedness Tremors or shakiness	Increased blood pressure Increased heart rate Headache Restlessness or anxiety Dizziness or lightheadedness Nausea or vomiting	Increased blood pressure Headache Nervousness or restlessness Dizziness Nausea or vomiting Difficulty sleeping	Increased heart rate Irregular heart rhythms Increased blood pressure. Headache Nausea or vomiting Anxiety or restlessness Tissue necrosis
Contra-indications	Known hypersensitivity to epinephrine or any of its components Myocardial infarction Angina pectoris Arrhythmias or Cardiomyopathy	Known hypersensitivity to norepinephrine or any of its components - Mesenteric or peripheral arterial vasoconstriction Hypovolemia	Phenylephrine is contraindicated in individuals with: Hypersensitivity or allergy to phenylephrine or any of its components Severe high blood pressure Severe coronary artery disease Closed-angle glaucoma	Dopamine is contraindicated in individuals with: Hypersensitivity or allergy to dopamine or any of its components. Pheochromocytoma Heart failure Occlusive peripheral vascular disorders Liver disease
Client Education Safety	Always carry prescribed epinephrine auto-injector with the client for allergic reactions.	Understand that norepinephrine is typically used in severe medical emergencies where the benefits outweigh the potential risks. Given only in the healthcare setting.	Use only the recommended dose and duration. If using nasal sprays or eye drops, make sure to clean the applicator tip before and after use to prevent contamination. Avoid using phenylephrine products alongside other medications that may raise blood pressure or cause similar side effects.	Dopamine is administered in a hospital or clinical setting by healthcare professionals. They will monitor the vital signs and adjust the dosage as necessary. Report any severe side effects or if the symptoms worsen. Do not stop or change the infusion without the guidance of a healthcare provider.

Sympathomimetics II

Drug	Dobutamine	Ephedrine	Isoproterenol
Route	Intravenous	IV, IM, Oral	IV, IM
Indications	Heart failure with reduced cardiac output. To assist in the management of acute heart conditions, such as acute decompensated heart failure or cardiogenic shock	Treatment of hypotension particularly in situations such as anesthesia, spinal anesthesia, or surgery where blood pressure may drop significantly. Management of bronchospasm (narrowing of the airways) in certain respiratory conditions, although this use is less common.	Indications: Isoproterenol is commonly used for: Treatment and management of various types of heart rhythm disorders, such as bradycardia (slow heart rate) or heart block.
Side Effects	Increased heart rate Irregular heart rhythms (arrhythmias) Increased blood pressure Headache Nausea or vomiting Tremors or shaking Chest pain or discomfort	Increased heart rate Increased blood pressure Restlessness or nervousness Headache Nausea or vomiting Dizziness or lightheadedness Difficulty sleeping (insomnia) Tremors or muscle twitching	Potential side effects of isoproterenol may include: Increased heart rate (tachycardia) Increased blood pressure Palpitations (abnormal awareness of the heartbeat) Headache Tremors or muscle twitching Nervousness or anxiety Flushing or sweating Chest pain Shortness of breath
Contra-indications	Hypersensitivity or allergy to dobutamine or any of its components. Hypertrophic obstructive cardiomyopathy Idiopathic hypertrophic subaortic stenosis Known or suspected low output states due to mechanical obstruction (e.g., aortic or pulmonic stenosis)	Hypersensitivity or allergy to ephedrine or any of its components Severe hypertension Ventricular tachycardia or arrhythmias Closed-angle glaucoma Hyperthyroidism Significant coronary artery disease or severe heart disease	Hypersensitivity or allergy to isoproterenol or any of its components. Uncontrolled hypertension Ventricular tachycardia or ventricular fibrillation Obstructive cardiomyopathy Acute myocardial infarction Pheochromocytoma Hyperthyroidism
Client Education Safety	Notify healthcare provider if there are any severe side effects, such as chest pain or significant changes in heart rate or blood pressure. Note increased urine output Do not take with metoprolol. Can cause a lower potassium level.	Interacts with caffeine Avoid in clients with angle closure glaucoma Do not mix with digoxin as the effectiveness of the medication may be decreased. This can be excreted in breastmilk.	This medication increases myocardial oxygen demands. May cause an increase in blood glucose levels in clients with diabetes mellitus.

Thyroid Medications

Drug	Levothyroxine	Liothyronine	Propylthiouracil	Methimazole
Route	Oral, IV, Rectal	Oral, IV	Oral	Oral
Indications	Primary, secondary, and tertiary hypothyroidism. Thyrotropin-dependent well-differentiated thyroid cancer	Hypothyroidism Goiter Test for hyperthyroidism	Hyperthyroidism Graves disease Multinodular goiter Radioactive iodine Thyrotoxicosis crisis	Grave's Disease Hyperthyroidism Thyroidectomy or radioactive iodine treatment
Side Effects	Weight gain or loss Headache, Vomiting Diarrhea Changes in appetite Fever Sensitivity to heat Hair loss Joint pain Leg cramps	Weight loss Nervousness Excessive sweating Sensitivity to heat Temporary hair loss Chest pain Rapid or irregular heartbeat or pulse	Black, tarry stools Chest pain Chills, Cough Fever, Painful urination Shortness of breath Sore throat, Swollen glands Unusual bruising Unusual tiredness	Black, tarry stools Bleeding Bloody or cloudy urine Burning, crawling, itching, numbness, "Pins and Needles" Chest pain Chills, Cough Dark urine Difficulty in breathing Constipation Depressed mood Dry skin and hair Feeling cold Muscle cramps Weight gain Unusual tiredness or weakness.
Contra-indications	Acute MI Adrenal insufficiency Acute myocarditis, Active cardiac Arrhythmias Thyrotoxicosis Hyperthyroidism	Hypersensitivity to thyroid hormone Acute MI Thyrotoxicosis, untreated adrenal insufficiency Treatment of obesity or infertility	Hypersensitivity Hepatic impairment Myelosuppression Pediatric patients.	Hypersensitivity Pregnancy Breastfeeding
Client Education **Safety**	Some meals and beverages, containing soybeans, walnuts, and dietary fiber, grapefruit, could affect levothyroxine functions. TSH levels in adults should be checked 6 to 8 weeks after starting levothyroxine. After establishing the appropriate levothyroxine dosing, TSH levels should be checked every 4 to 6 months, and subsequently every 12 months.	Thyroid hormone should not be given for weight loss if the client has normal thyroid function, Liothyronine combined with amphetamines can be life threatening. Liothyronine may also interact with various other drugs. Pregnant and breastfeeding clients should inform their doctor if taking these medications.	Monitor thyroid function test and PTT while the client is on PTU therapy. Propylthiouracil can temporarily reduce the WBCs, increasing the risk of infection. Difficult or painful urinating may occur. Report any unusual bleeding or bruises. It is the antithyroid medication of choice in the first trimester of pregnancy.	If the client is pregnant, intends to become pregnant, or is nursing, they should see a doctor. Methimazole may upset the stomach. Methimazole should be taken with food or milk.

Psychiatric Medication Section

Drug	Benzodiazepines
Route	Oral, IV, Nasal
Indications	Anxiety disorders, Insomnia, Acute status epilepticus, Induction of amnesia, Spastic disorders Seizure disorders, Agitation, Alcohol withdrawal, Preoperative and procedural sedation
Side Effects	Respiratory depression, Respiratory arrest, Drowsiness, Confusion, Headache, Syncope, Nausea/vomiting Diarrhea, Tremor
Contra-indications	Hypersensitivity Angle-closure glaucoma Respiratory depression (COPD, respiratory failure) Myasthenia gravis History of a substance use disorder (e.g., alcohol, recreational drugs, prescription medications) Pregnancy, Severe hepatic and renal impairment
Client Education Safety	Benzodiazepines are CNS depressants that block respiratory drive particularly. As a result, after the administration of benzodiazepines, all vital signs, particularly blood pressure and respiration rate, should be carefully monitored. Benzodiazepines should be given with extreme caution in elderly patients since they can worsen cognitive impairment, increase the risk of falls, and induce paradoxical reactions. Many drug interactions can occur with benzodiazepines; therefore, a drug interaction screen performed by a healthcare provider is an important step each time a new drug is added or stopped in any treatment plan.

non-Benzodiazepines

Drug	Buspirone	Zolpidem
Route	Oral	Oral Sublingual
Indications	Generalized anxiety disorder (GAD). Used to relieve symptoms such as excessive worry, restlessness, irritability and tension.	Short-term treatment of insomnia, specifically for difficulty falling asleep. It helps initiate and maintain sleep.
Side Effects	Dizziness, Drowsiness, Nausea or upset stomach Headache, Dry mouth, Nervousness or excitement Blurred vision, Difficulty sleeping	Daytime drowsiness, Dizziness or lightheadedness Headache Nausea Diarrhea or constipation Dry mouth, Muscle pain **Memory problems or confusion Behavioral or mood changes such as aggression, agitation, or hallucinations
Contra-indications	Hypersensitivity: Should not be used in individuals with a known hypersensitivity to the drug or its components. <u>Concomitant Use with Monoamine Oxidase Inhibitors</u> (MAOIs): Should not be used within 14 days of discontinuing treatment with a MAOI, as it can lead to a potentially dangerous increase in blood pressure.	Hypersensitivity: Zolpidem should not be used in individuals with a known hypersensitivity to the drug Impaired respiratory function. Sleep Apnea: unless they are using appropriate continuous positive airway pressure (CPAP). Myasthenia Gravis: May worsen muscle weakness in individuals Dependence or Substance Abuse: Zolpidem can be habit-forming.
Client Education Safety	May be taken with or without food. Avoid grapefruit juice as it can interact with grapefruit or grapefruit juice, leading to increased levels of the medication in the body.	Alcohol should be avoided while taking zolpidem as it can increase the sedative effects of the medication and impair coordination and judgment. Zolpidem is indicated for short-term use only, generally for a duration of 7 to 10 days. Prolonged use may lead to dependence or tolerance.

Psychiatric Medication Section

Drug	Lithium Carbonate
Route	Oral (Capsule / Solution/ Tablet)
Indications	Bipolar disorder Aggression, post-traumatic stress disorder, Conduct disorder in children, augmented agent for depression. Currently being studied for improvement of neutrophil counts in clients with cancer chemotherapy—induced neutropenia and as prophylaxis of cluster headaches and migraine headaches; not recommended for children 12 years.
Side Effects	Occasional: Fine hand tremor, polydipsia, polyuria, mild nausea. Rare: Weight gain, bradycardia, tachycardia, acne, rash, muscle twitching, peripheral cyanosis, pseudotumor cerebri (eye pain, headache, tinnitus, vision disturbances Lithium Toxicity : Lithium serum concentration of 1.5–2.0 mEq/L may produce vomiting, diarrhea, drowsiness, confusion, incoordination, coarse hand tremor, muscle twitching, T-wave depression on EKG. Lithium serum concentration of 2.0–2.5 mEq/L may result in ataxia, giddiness, tinnitus, blurred vision, clonic movements, severe hypotension. Acute toxicity may be characterized by seizures, oliguria, circulatory failure, coma, death.
Contra-indications	Clients with significant renal or cardiac disease that could be exacerbated by the toxic effects of the drug. Clients with a history of leukemia, metabolic disorders, including sodium depletion, dehydration, and diuretic use. (Lithium depletes sodium reabsorption, and severe hyponatremia may occur.) Pregnancy and lactation are also contraindications because of the potential for adverse effects on the fetus or neonate
Client Education Safety	Administer drug with food or milk to alleviate GI irritation. Recommend clients to maintain adequate intake of salt and fluid to decrease toxicity. Arrange for small, frequent meals, sugarless lozenges to suck, and frequent mouth care, to increase secretions and decrease discomfort as needed. Provide thorough patient teaching, including drug name, prescribed dosage, measures for avoidance of adverse effects, cautions that it may take time to see the desired therapeutic effect, warning signs that may indicate possible problems, and the need to avoid pregnancy while taking lithium to enhance patient knowledge about drug therapy and to promote compliance. **The therapeutically effective serum level is 0.6 to 1.2 mEq/L.** Monitor serum sodium because hyponatremia leads to lithium retention and toxicity. Breast-feeding should be discontinued while using lithium. A lithium– haloperidol combination may result in an encephalopathic syndrome, consisting of weakness, lethargy, confusion, tremors, extrapyramidal symptoms, leukocytosis, and irreversible brain damage. If lithium is given with carbamazepine, increased CNS toxicity may occur, and a lithium–iodide salt combination results in an increased risk of hypothyroidism.

Typical Antipsychotics

Drug	Thorazine	Compazine	Stelazine	Promethazine	Haloperidol	Chlorpromazine
Route	Oral, IM, or IV	Oral, IM, or IV	Oral	Oral, Rectal, IM, IV	Oral, IM, or IV	Oral, IM, IV, Rectal
Indications	Schizophrenia **Positive signs** Bipolar disorder To control N/V Chronic hiccups Acute porphyria	Schizophrenia Generalized non-psychotic anxiety	Schizophrenia Psychosis Short-term management of anxiety Nausea and vomiting	Allergic conditions Nausea and vomiting Motion sickness Sedation	Schizophrenia Tourette disorder Hyperactivity Anxiety Hallucinations Delusions	Schizophrenia Bipolar I acute Persistent singultus Apprehension before surgery
Side Effects	Allergic reactions Infection High prolactin level Liver injury Hypotension Extrapyramidal symptoms	Drowsiness Lightheadedness Blurred vision Constipation Dry mouth Nausea/Vomiting Mental/mood changes Bleeding Bruising Signs of infection Jaundice	Difficulty urinating Decreased cough reflex Edema Butterfly-shaped rash on nose and cheeks Joint pain Skin discoloration Vision changes Jaundices Signs of anemia Mental/mood changes.	Drowsiness Dizziness Ringing in ears Double vision Nervousness Dry mouth Tiredness Insomnia Allergic reaction: Hives Difficulty breathing Swelling of the face, lips, tongue, or throat.	Difficulty speaking or swallowing Inability to move the eyes Loss of balance control Mask-like face Muscle spasms Shuffling walk Stiffness Twisting movements	Extrapyramidal symptoms-EPS the following are the side effects: Feelings of anxiety Agitation Jitteriness Drooling Shaking (tremor) Shuffling walk Spasms Mask-like expression of the face.
Contra-indications	History of allergic reactions Do not give with CNS depressants Clients with a poorly controlled seizure disorder.	Allergy to prochlorperazine or the phenothiazine drug class. History of seizure/epilepsy Narrow-angle glaucoma Prostatic hypertrophy Past or current history of tardive dyskinesia Clients under two years of age.	Hypersensitivity CNS depression Coma Blood dyscrasias	Hypersensitivity Children under two years of age Comatose clients Clients with lower respiratory tract symptoms Contraindicated for subcutaneous or intra-arterial administration due to the risk of tissue damage.	Allergic reactions Parkinson disease Dementia with Lewy body Comatose patients Severe central nervous system (CNS) depression Concurrent use with CNS depressants.	Hypersensitivity to phenothiazines. Clients with a poorly controlled seizure disorder. Clients taking SSRIs such as citalopram and escitalopram. The drug should be used cautiously in clients on: Antihypertensive medications.
Client Education Safety	It reduces symptoms like hallucinations, delusions, and agitation. May cause photosensitivity Do not take with alcohol. Antacids, antihistamines, or certain antidepressants may interact	Notify MD of movement changes (such as fixed upward stare, neck twisting, tongue movements, muscle spasms) Shaking Difficulty urinating.	Twitching or uncontrollable movements of the eyes, lips, tongue, face, arms, or legs; tremors. This may indicate tardive dyskinesia.	Monitor for respiratory depression. Photosensitivity May cause neuroleptic malignant syndrome (NMS). May affect blood glucose levels.	Medication may cause overheating resulting in heat stroke. Haloperidol may cause photo-sensitivity avoid sun between 10:00 a.m. and 3:00 p.m., if possible.	QT prolongation may occur.

Atypical Antipsychotics

Drug	Clozapine	Risperidone	Aripiprazole	Olanzapine	Quetiapine
Route	Oral	Oral, IM, SC	Oral, IM	Oral, IM	Oral
Indications	Schizophrenia, Bipolar mania. Suicidal behavior Schizoaffective disorders.	Bipolar disorder Schizophrenia. Mania Delusional disorder Tourette syndrome	Schizophrenia, Bipolar disorder. Major depressive disorder Autistic disorder in children 6–17 yrs. of age. Tourette's syndrome	Schizophrenia Acute mania of bipolar disorder.	Schizophrenia Acute manic episodes Acute depression Psychosis/agitation related to Alzheimer's dementia
Side Effects	Drowsiness, Constipation. hypotension, headache, tremor, syncope Dry mouth, Visual disturbances, Nightmares, Weight gain Metabolic disorders Severe neutropenia, orthostatic	Agitation, anxiety insomnia, headache, constipation dyspepsia, rhinitis, rash, abdominal pain, dry skin, tachycardia, visual disturbances, fever, back pain, pharyngitis, cough,	Weight gain, headache, insomnia, vomiting, light-headedness, nausea, vision, constipation, asthenia, anxiety, fever, rash, cough, rhinitis, and orthostatic hypotension agranulocytosis.	Drowsiness, agitation, insomnia, headache, nervousness, hostility, dizziness, rhinitis. Constipation, nonaggressive atypical behavior, dry mouth, weight gain, orthostatic hypotension	Headache, drowsiness, dizziness, constipation, orthostatic hypotension, tachycardia, dry mouth, fever, weight gain.
Contra-indications	Clozapine induced agranulocytosis Myeloproliferative disorders Concomitant use with bone marrow suppressants Hepatic disease Paralytic ileus Cardiac disease Renal failure	Medication should not be given via IV route. Renal/hepatic impairment Seizure disorders Cardiac disease, Narrow-angle glaucoma clients with high risk of suicide.	Contraindicated to clients with hypersensitivity to aripiprazole. Use with caution in clients with cardiovascular disease, Parkinson's disease and seizures, Agranulocytosis may occur.	Contraindicated to clients with hypersensitivity to olanzapine. Hyperprolactinemia Suicidal ideations, Cardiovascular diseases decreased GI motility Liver disease Parkinson's disease and seizures.	Contraindicated in clients with hypersensitivity to quetiapine Precaution in clients with cancer, decreased GI motility, hepatic impairment, seizures, and urinary retention.
Client Education Safety	Discourage abrupt discontinuing long-term drug therapy, tasks that require alertness, motor skills until response to drug is found. Avoid alcohol and caffeine. Teach the client to report fever, sore throat, flu-like symptoms. Monitor blood pressure for hypotension / hypertension. Monitor CBC for blood dyscrasias.	Educate client to avoid tasks that may require alertness, motor skills until response to drug is established. Teach clients to report trembling in fingers, altered gait, unusual movements. Serum renal and liver function should be performed before therapy begins. Obtain fasting serum glucose.	Discourage use of alcohol and avoid tasks that require alertness, motor skills until response to drug is established. Teach client to report worsening of depression or suicidal ideation. Monitor for tardive dyskinesia	Encouraged clients to hydrate well and avoid dehydration, May use sugarless gum, sips of water may relieve dry mouth. Report suspected pregnancy. Obtain baseline liver function test, Supervise suicidal-risk patients closely during early therapy.	Discourage exposure to extreme heat. Avoid tasks that require alertness, motor skills until response to drug is established. Avoid alcohol. Slowly go from lying to standing. Report suicidal ideation and unusual changes in behavior. Eye exam to detect cataract formation should be obtained every 6 months during treatment.

Thyroid Hormones

	Thyroid Replacement Hormone	Anti-thyroid agent
Generic Names	Levothyroxine Liothyronine	Propylthiouracil Methimazole
Indication	Hypothyroidism Bind to thyroid receptors on the surface of body cells to mimic the actions of thyroid hormones	Hyperthyroidism
Side Effects	Headache, insomnia, nervousness, tachycardia, palpitations, cardiac arrest, weight loss, excessive sweating, heat intolerance, and thyroid crisis	Headache, goiter, gastrointestinal disturbances, hepatitis, jaundice, nephritis, lymphadenopathy, leukopenia, thrombocytopenia, bleeding, vasculitis, skin rash, urticaria, pruritus, arthralgia, myalgia, and muscle cramps (propylthiouracil): hepatotoxicity, severe liver injury, acute liver failure
Contra-indications	Thyrotoxicosis	Pregnancy and breastfeeding Use with caution in infants, bone marrow depression, bleeding disorders, and leukopenia
Client Education Safety	Take with plenty of water on an empty stomach at least 30 to 60 minutes before breakfast three to four hours before other medication, e.g., acid reducing medications, supplements with calcium or iron **DO NOT STOP abruptly** **Lifelong hormone replacement** therapy required. Recognize and **report symptoms** of hyperthyroidism: *rapid pulse, palpitations, chest pain, tremor, trouble sleeping, weight loss, heat intolerance.* Self-monitor pulse	Take each day, at the **same time** every day Can take several weeks to normalize thyroid levels. Do not stop abruptly. Female clients: use reliable birth control; contact healthcare provider if pregnant. Recognize and report symptoms of Hypothyroidism Blood dyscrasias Liver dysfunction

Vaccinations

	Inactivated Vaccines	Live-Attenuated Vaccines	Messenger RNA (mRNA) Vaccines	Subunit, recombinant, polysaccharide, and conjugate vaccines	Toxoid Vaccines	Viral Vector Vaccines
Generic Names	Hepatitis A – two doses Influenza - yearly Japanese encephalitis – two doses Polio – four doses Rabies – 3 doses Typhoid – single dose	Chickenpox (varicella) vaccines FluMist - intranasal MMR vaccines Rotavirus vaccines Yellow fever vaccine	COVID-19	Hib (Haemophilus influenzae type b) disease Hepatitis B HPV (Human papillomavirus) Whooping cough Pneumococcal disease Meningococcal disease Shingles	Diphtheria Tetanus	COVID-19 Ebola
Indications	These vaccines use the killed pathogens that cause the infection. Inactivated vaccines do not provide strong protection as compared to live vaccines.	Live vaccines contain a weakened form of the pathogen that causes the infection. This makes the immunity stronger and long-lasting because of its similarity to the natural infection.	mRNA vaccines that produce proteins that stimulate an immune response. They have several advantages compared to other type of vaccines. They have shorter manufacturing times.	These vaccines contain specific parts of pathogens that cause the disease. Because it is specific, it gives a very strong immunity that is also target-specific. This is also safe to use for immune-compromised clients.	Uses a toxin produced by the pathogen that causes the disease. This produces immunity from the part of the pathogen and not by the pathogen itself. Therefore, the immune response is targeted to the pathogen's toxin only.	Viral vector vaccines containing a modified version of a different pathogen as a vector to provide immunity. Examples of viruses are influenza, measles, VSV, and adenovirus, which cause common colds.
Side Effects	Inflammation at the injection site Anorexia Fever Tinnitus	Inflammation at the injection site Fever myalgia FluMist may cause upper respiratory symptoms	Injection site: redness soreness Swelling chills fatigue joint pain headache mild fever muscle aches	Pain/tenderness redness and swelling at the injection site fatigue muscle pain headache joint pain nausea/vomiting fever	Pain, redness, or swelling at the injection site Fever Headache or other body aches Tiredness Nausea, vomiting or diarrhea Hives Difficulty breathing	Pain at the injection site fatigue headache fever Chills muscle pain and joint pain
Safety Teaching	Some inactivated vaccines should be given for several doses to be fully protected especially on high-risk individuals.	Clients like organ transplant recipients, HIV, cancer, and autoimmune disorders should not be given live vaccines.	mRNA vaccines usually require two shots, Immunocompromised persons might need to get the third dose.	This type of vaccine may require booster shots for continuous protection from the disease. Immuno-compromised individuals who cannot receive the live vaccines can take these.	Toxoid vaccines may also require booster shots to provide strong immunity from the disease.	Viral vector vaccines commonly provide strong immunity from infection. A single dose is typically enough to develop immunity.

 Study more at ReMarNurse.com | Join live weekly on YouTube @ReMarNurse

Vitamins and Minerals

Drug	Calcium	Iodine	Iron
Route	Oral, IV	Oral	Oral, IV
Indications	Osteoporosis/ Osteomalacia Hypocalcemic conditions Hypoparathyroidism Hyperkalemia Premenstrual syndrome	Iodine deficiency Exposure to radiation Fetal neurodevelopment Fibrocystic breast disease	Iron deficiency anemia Anemia due to pregnancy Heart failure
Side Effects	Gas in stomach Constipation Bloating	Metallic taste Soreness of teeth and gums Burning in mouth and throat Stomach upset	Stomach upset & Heartburn Nausea/Vomiting/ Diarrhea Loss of appetite Dark stool
Contra-indications	Hypersensitivity Renal impairment or chronic kidney disease (CKD) History of calcium-containing kidney stones.	Hypersensitivity Nodular thyroid conditions with cardiac disease. Current or history of thyrotoxicosis Nodular goiter Latent Graves' disease Adrenal insufficiency Acute bronchitis Tuberculosis Thyroid cancer Acute dehydration Heat cramp	Hypersensitivity Hemochromatosis Hemosiderosis With history of hemolytic anemia Parenteral iron: Untreated pyelonephritis Acute liver disease
Client Education Safety	Calcium supplements can interact with prescribed medication, such as blood pressure medications, synthetic thyroid hormones, bisphosphonates, antibiotics, and calcium channel blockers. Calcium may reduce the effectiveness of other medications. Do not take calcium carbonate within 1-2 hours of taking other medications. Rapid IV infusion can cause cardiac arrest, monitor the client's blood pressure and pulse.	Thyroid function tests should be monitored, especially in pregnant women, children, and newborns. Examine for signs and symptoms of hyperthyroidism. Iodine supplements may interact with various drugs, including potassium-sparing diuretics, ACE inhibitors, and anti-thyroid drugs.	If using a tablet form, swallow the tablet whole. Don't try to crush, chew or break it. If liquid form, use a dosing syringe to measure, not a kitchen spoon to get an accurate dose of the medication. The supplement works best on an empty stomach, but it is recommended take it with food so it doesn't upset the stomach. Do not take iron supplements with milk, caffeine, antacids or calcium supplements. For better absorption, take iron supplement with vitamin C (for example, a glass of orange juice).
Food sources	Dairy products, such as cheese, milk and yogurt. Dark green leafy vegetables, such as broccoli and kale. Fish with edible soft bones, such as sardines and canned salmon Calcium-fortified foods and beverages, such as soy products, cereal and fruit juices, and milk substitutes.	Seaweed (nori, kelp, kombu, wakame) Fish, shellfish (cod, canned tuna, oysters, shrimp) Table salts labeled "iodized." Dairy (milk, cheese, yogurt) Eggs Beef liver Chicken Fortified infant formula	Lean meat and poultry. Seafood such as salmon. White beans, kidney beans, lentils and peas. Nuts and dried fruits. Green leafy vegetables such as spinach. Fortified bread and breakfast cereals.

Vitamins and Minerals

Drug	Vitamin A	Vitamin C	Vitamin D	Vitamin E	Vitamin K
Route	Oral	Oral, IV, IM	Oral, IV, Topical	Oral, Topical	Oral, IV (Vitamin K1)
Indications	Fetal development Cystic fibrosis Inflammatory bowel disease Acne, Eye health Cancer Measles Vitamin A deficiency	Vitamin C deficiency Scurvy, Heart Disease High Blood Pressure Common Cold Cancer, Osteoarthritis Age-related Macular Degeneration Pre-eclampsia Asthma	Vitamin D Deficiency Hypoparathyroidism Refractory rickets Multiple sclerosis Osteomalacia Osteoporosis Psoriasis	Vitamin E deficiency Ataxia with vitamin E deficiency Alzheimer disease Beta-thalassemia	Vitamin K deficiency Hypoprothrombinemia Reveresing the effects of blood thinners
Side Effects	Nausea/ Vomiting Vertigo Blurry vision Liver damage Headache **Skin irritation Painful joints/bones Birth defects	GI Upset Heartburn Stomach cramps Fatigue Insomnia Headache Skin flushing	Weakness Dry mouth Nausea/ Vomiting Constipation Arrhythmias Kidney stones	Nausea/ Diarrhea Intestinal cramps Fatigue Headache Blurred vision Creatinuria	Decreased appetite Difficulty in breathing Enlarged liver Edema Irritability Muscle stiffness Paleness Yellow eyes or skin
Contra-indications	Hypersensitivity Fat absorption disorders Celiac disease Cystic fibrosis Pancreatic disease Cirrhosis of the liver Pregnancy as this medication can cause birth defects.	Blood disorders like thalassemia, sickle cell disease, and hemochromatosis. Immediately before or following angioplasty Diabetes Clients having kidney stones	Hypersensitivity Hypercalcemia Gastrointestinal (GI), liver, or biliary disease associated with malabsorption of vitamin D analogs	Vitamin K deficiency Retinitis pigmentosa Bleeding disorders Diabetes Heart attack Stroke Liver disease	Hypersensitivity to vitamin K Hereditary hypoprothrombinemia Renal impairment Cases of over anticoagulation
Client Education Safety	Drinking alcohol may exacerbate effects of vitamin A on the liver. May increase triglycerides in the blood.	Vitamin C supplements have a diuretic effect. Vitamin C levels are decreased by smoking and chewing tobacco. Vitamin C may increase blood glucose levels in diabetics.	Sunlight is the most common source of vitamin D for most people. Phenobarbital, phenytoin, & other anticonvulsants may increase the use of vitamin D.	Interacts with anticoagulants Interferes with beta blockers. If using topically do not get into the eyes.	Prothrombin time (PT) and INR are typically used to evaluate vitamin K dose or levels, particularly in clients with warfarin toxicity or vitamin K-related coagulopathies.
Food sources	Types of fish, such as herring and salmon, Beef liver and other organ meats. Green leafy vegetables such as spinach, sweet potatoes, carrots, and broccoli. Fruits, including cantaloupe, mangos, and apricots Dairy products, such as milk and cheese.	Cantaloupe Citrus fruit, Grapefruit, Kiwi fruit Mango, Papaya Pineapple, Strawberries, raspberries, blueberries, and cranberries Green and red peppers, Spinach, Cabbage, turnip greens, and other leafy greens Sweet potatoes Tomatoes	Cod liver oil Salmon Swordfish Tuna fish Orange juice fortified with vitamin D Dairy and plant milks fortified with vitamin D Sardines Beef liver Egg yolk Fortified cereals	Wheat Germ Oil Almonds Sunflower Seeds Pine Nuts Avocado Peanut Butter Fish Red Bell Peppers	Green leafy vegetables including collard and turnip greens, kale, spinach, broccoli, Brussels sprouts, cabbage, lettuces Soybean and canola oil Salad dressings made with soybean or canola oil Fortified meal replacement shakes

Vitamins and Minerals

Drug	Vitamin B1 Thiamin	Vitamin B2 Riboflavin	Vitamin B3 Niacin	Vitamin B5 Pantothenic acid	Vitamin B6	Vitamin B7 Biotin	Folate and Folic Acid	Vitamin B12
Route	Oral, IV, IM	Oral	Oral	Oral	Oral, IV	Oral	Oral, IM, SC	Oral, IM, IV
Indications	Thiamine deficiency Beriberi Wernicke-Korsakoff syndrome Menstrual cramps Alcoholism	Riboflavin deficiency Hyper-homocysteinemia Health of digestive tract	High cholesterol Niacin deficiency (pellagra)	Pantothenic acid deficiency Malnutrition Wound healing Radiation dermatitis	Vitamin B6 deficiency Pyridoxine-dependent epilepsy	Vitamin B7 deficiency Multiple sclerosis Seborrheic dermatitis	Macrocytic anemia Alcoholism Malabsorption disorders Pregnancy	Anemia Gastrectomy Helicobacter pylori infection Deficiency of Vitamin B12 Crohn's disease Celiac disease Alcoholism
Side Effects	Flushing Hives Itching Weakness Sweating Nausea Restlessness	Skin rash Itching Hives Swelling of the face, lips, tongue, or throat	Skin flushing Dizziness Tachycardia Itching N/V Abdominal pain Diarrhea Gout Liver damage	Muscle pain Diabetes mellitus Flu-like symptoms Nausea Abdominal pain Increased (ALT) Constipation Flulike illness UTI	Nausea Stomach pain Loss of appetite Headache Ataxia Painful Skin lesions Numbness	Insomnia Acne GI upset Skin rashes Excessive thirst Kidney problems	Bad taste in mouth Nausea Loss of appetite Confusion Irritability Sleep pattern disturbance Skin rash Difficulty breathing	Mild diarrhea Itching Skin rash Headache Dizziness N/V Pulmonary edema CHF Thrombosis Polycythemia vera
Contra-indications	Allergic reactions	Allergic reactions	Liver problems Peptic ulcer disease hypotension	Allergic reactions	Allergic reactions	Allergic reactions	Allergic reactions	Allergy reactions Renal failure
Client Education Safety	Give thiamine before glucose as it helps with absorption.	Bright yellow urine is normal and expected. Patient should report sore or swollen throat.	Do not combine with alcohol. Do not give to client with gout. May affect blood sugar levels tests has been observed.	Mixing with blood-thinners warfarin aspirin, and others since high dosages of vitamin B5 might exacerbate bleeding.	Take in the morning instead of night. Do not take with levodopa.	It may react with other medication like antipsychotic drugs, antidepressant and muscle relaxants. Interferes with thyroid function tests.	May interact with epilepsy medications, methotrexate, and sulfasalazine.	After having a coronary stent, avoid combining vitamin B12, folate, and vitamin B6.
Food sources	Whole grains Brown rice Pork-is the highest source of thiamine.	Dairy products Eggs Beef Organ meats Almonds Spinach	Red meat Pork Poultry Fish Brown rice Legumes Bananas	Broccoli Cabbage Sweet potatoes Whole-grain cereals Mushrooms Nuts	Chickpeas Beef Organ Meats Potatoes Banana Tofu Nuts	Egg yolk Organ meats (liver, kidney) Nuts Soybeans and other legumes Whole grains Bananas Mushrooms	Dark green leafy vegetables Peanuts Sunflower seeds Fresh fruits, Whole grains Liver, Eggs	Beef, Pork Ham Poultry Lamb, Fish Dairy products, milk, cheese, and yogurt

Quick Facts for Nursing School Practice Quiz

Are you ready to put your knowledge to the test?

1. Which opportunistic infections is **most** likely to cause blindness in A.I.D.S. patients with a CD4 count of less than 200?

    1. Cytomegalovirus
    2. Cryptosporidiosis
    3. Histoplasmosis
    4. Pneumocystis pneumonia

2. A 65-yr-old elderly man presents to the eye clinic and is seen by the nurse. The patient complains of a single floater in his peripheral vision and brief flashes of light. The nurse is aware the patient may be suffering from what?

    1. Diabetic retinopathy
    2. Detached retina
    3. Enucleation
    4. Cataracts

3. A 4-year-old client who is frequently admitted to the emergency room is diagnosed with acute otitis media. The nurse knows which part of the ear is inflamed?

    1. Middle
    2. Inner media
    3. External Os
    4. Conductive Os

4. Who should the nurse see **first**?

    1. A male client with hypothyroidism reports fatigue.
    2. A male client with hypothyroidism who needs suctioning.
    3. A male client with hypothyroidism who needs a dressing change.
    4. A male client with hypothyroidism complaining of moderate pain.

5. A client is just returning from surgery. The client reports a total thyroidectomy; her calcium level is 6.0. Which finding would cause the **most** concern for the nurse caring for this patient?

    1. Laryngospasms
    2. Muscle spasms
    3. Persistent diarrhea
    4. Facial tremors

6. A client has been diagnosed with Meniere's disease. She has frequent attacks of vertigo and tinnitus. The nurse is aware which of the following is the **best** diet for the client?

    1. Low sodium
    2. Low protein
    3. High calorie
    4. High carbohydrate

7. A nurse cares for a client with a recent liver transplant. The client has become unstable and breathing has stopped. The nurse is unable to find a pulse and emergency interventions are necessary. Which task is **most** appropriate to delegate to a unlicensed personnel?

   1. Give rescue breaths during cardiopulmonary resuscitation.
   2. Assist with oral intubation.
   3. Administer epinephrine IM.
   4. Place the transcutaneous pacing pads.

8. A mother calls into the wellness center and states that her 7-year-old daughter has been stung by a honeybee. The nurse is on the phone to give advice to the situation. Which action should the nurse tell the mother to perform **first**?

   1. Administer diphenhydramine to reduce allergic response.
   2. Hang up the phone and dial 911.
   3. Take the child's temperature and monitor respirations.
   4. Remove the stinger by scraping the skin.

9. After receiving change of shift report at 7:00 AM, which client should the nurse assess **first**?

   1. A 13-yr-old with a migraine headache who is reporting severe nausea associated with dry heaving.
   2. A 40-yr-old who is scheduled for an EGD in 30 minutes and needs pre-operative teaching.
   3. A 49-yr-old patient with Parkinson's disease who will need a swallowing assessment before breakfast.
   4. A 60-yr-old patient with multiple sclerosis with an oral temperature of 101.6 Fahrenheit (38.6) and back pain.

10. A nurse is caring for a client with a diagnosis of syndrome of inappropriate antidiuretic hormone secretion (SIADH). Which electrolyte imbalance should the nurse expect?

    1. Hypernatremia
    2. Hypokalemia
    3. Hyperkalemia
    4. Hyponatremia

11. The nurse is caring for a client newly diagnosed with AIDS. She demonstrates when taking blood samples to use which isolation precaution?

    1. Respiratory
    2. Contact
    3. Droplet
    4. Universal

12. A patient has received teaching for her 4-year-old diagnosed with HIV. Which of the following statements need follow-up teaching? Select all that apply.

    1. I should not wash my child's eating utensils in the dishwasher with family dishes.
    2. It is ok to kiss my child's hands, wrists, mouth, and cheeks.
    3. I will cover any uneaten food of my child's and place it in the refrigerator.
    4. I will monitor my child's weight.
    5. I will make sure to take out the trash on a weekly basis.

13. Which of the following clients is at greatest risk for developing acute renal failure? Select all that apply.

    1. A client who has been diagnosed with renal artery occlusion.
    2. A client who has been diagnosed with diabetes insipidus.
    3. A client who has been diagnosed with hypertension.
    4. A client who has been diagnosed with diabetes mellitus.
    5. A client who has been diagnosed with gestational diabetes.

14. A client has just been given a medication that they are allergic to. Which is the priority action of the nurse?

    1. Write a note in the client's chart.
    2. Notify the physician.
    3. Place an allergy band on the client.
    4. Notify the family of the incident.

15. A nurse is starting her shift. Which patient should she see first?

    1. A 43-year-old patient who just started gentamycin with a temperature of 101.
    2. A 65-year-old patient reporting gastric upset who is taking clindamycin.
    3. A 70-year-old patient who has just started furosemide along with her vancomycin.
    4. A 19-years -old patient and just prescribed telithromycin.

16. Trimethoprim-sulfamethoxazole is prescribed for a patient. Before giving this medication the nurse knows to assess for which common adverse reaction?

    1. Stevens-Johnson syndrome
    2. Pseudomembranous colitis
    3. Sjogren's syndrome
    4. Stockholm syndrome

17. A client is diagnosed with systemic lupus erythematosus. Which of the following is a classic sign?

    1. Skin lesions on the face
    2. Bronchospasms
    3. Blood clots
    4. Difficulty swallowing

18. Raynaud's disease is which of the following?

    1. Acute encephalopathy
    2. Vasospasm of the arteries of the upper and lower extremities
    3. Sustained hypertension
    4. Decreased oxygenation in joints of the hands

19. A patient presents to the community health clinic with chancres on the genital area. Which of the following should be documented by the nurse.

    1. Gonorrhea; primary stage
    2. Genital herpes; tertiary stage
    3. Chlamydia; tertiary stage
    4. Syphilis; primary stage

20. A nurse is reading the doctor's orders for a patient who is expected to receive a tracheostomy. Which of the following is an indication for this surgery?

    1. Pneumonia
    2. A stoma
    3. Need for oxygen use
    4. Airway obstruction

21. Which of the following is responsible for eye movement?

    1. Cranial nerve VII
    2. Cranial nerve IV
    3. Cranial nerve X
    4. Cranial nerve XII

22. Which of the following is a complication of anorexia?

    1. abdominal fistula
    2. skin rashes
    3. cardiac arrhythmia
    4. thrombocytopenia

23. Which of the following should be considered an expected side effect of COPD? Select all that apply.

    1. Weight gain
    2. Clubbed fingers
    3. Barrel chest
    4. Dyspnea
    5. Diabetes mellitus type 2

24. Which of the following is a sign of newborn hypoglycemia?

   1. Apnea
   2. Jaundice
   3. Abdominal pain
   4. Dizziness

25. Which of the following is considered an elevated hyperbilirubinemia?

   1. 10 mg/ dl.
   2. 4 mg/ dl.
   3. 0.7 mg/ dl.
   4. 15 mg/dl.

26. Which of the following can be prescribed in pregnancy to treat genital herpes?

   1. Antibiotic therapy
   2. Acyclovir
   3. Allopurinol
   4. Sildenafil

27. What is the main treatment of polycythemia vera?

   1. Vancomycin
   2. Plasma transplants
   3. Phlebotomy
   4. Albumin infusion

28.The nurse notes inflammation of a vein. Which term should she document?

   1. Extravasation
   2. Infiltration
   3. Laminectomy
   4. Phlebitis

29. Pheochromocytoma is a disorder of which gland?

   1. Kidneys
   2. Brain
   3. Thyroid
   4. Adrenal

30. A 5-year-old child with asthma is wheezing and experiencing respiratory distress. What action should the registered nurse take first?

   1. Administer the prescribed bronchodilator.
   2. Start oxygen therapy.
   3. Document the findings.
   4. Notify the healthcare provider.

31. A 9-year-old child is admitted with suspected appendicitis. What assessment finding should the registered nurse report immediately to the healthcare provider?

   1. Decreased bowel sounds
   2. Low-grade fever
   3. Rebound tenderness in the right lower quadrant
   4. Increased appetite

32. A 2-year-old child with suspected dehydration presents to the emergency room. The nurse should prioritize which assessment finding related to dehydration?

   1. Heart rate
   2. Temperature
   3. Respiratory rate
   4. Blood pressure

33. A client with a history of COPD presents to the emergency department with bronchiolitis. What intervention for the registered nurse is essential for RSV infection control?

   1. Strict enteric precautions
   2. Airborne precautions
   3. Contact precautions
   4. Droplet precautions

34. A 23-year-old client is admitted with diabetic ketoacidosis (DKA). What acid base imbalance should the nurse anticipate in this young adult?

    1. metabolic acidosis
    2. metabolic alkalosis
    3. respiratory acidosis
    4. respiratory alkalosis

35. A nurse is caring for patient with hyperthyroidism. What physical manifestation should the nurse anticipate in the findings?

    1. Fatigue and lethargy
    2. Weight gain and constipation
    3. Bradycardia
    4. Increased heart rate and restlessness

36. A client with diabetes insipidus is experiencing excessive thirst and urination. What medication should the nurse expect to administer to manage this condition?

    1. Regular insulin
    2. Levothyroxine
    3. Desmopressin
    4. Glucagon

37. A client with diabetes insipidus is scheduled for a follow-up diagnostic exam. Which diagnostic test is most appropriate to identify the underlying cause of this condition?

    1. Blood glucose level
    2. T3 and T4 level
    3. Serum electrolyte level
    4. Urine specific gravity

38. A client diagnosed with deep vein thrombosis (DVT) is receiving enoxaparin. Which action should the nurse prioritize?

    1. Monitor serum potassium levels
    2. Assess blood glucose levels
    3. Measure the INR
    4. Check for signs of bleeding

39. A client with hypertension is prescribed lisinopril, an angiotensin-converting enzyme inhibitor. The nurse should instruct the client to monitor for which potential adverse effect of this medication?

    1. hyperkalemia
    2. dry cough
    3. hypoglycemia
    4. hypertension exacerbation

40. A client with atrial fibrillation is prescribed warfarin. The nurse should instruct the client to monitor which laboratory value for the therapeutic effect of the medication.

    1. Platelet count
    2. PT and INR
    3. Partial thromboplastin time
    4. Fibrinogen levels

41. A client is experiencing chest pain and shortness of breath. Upon assessment the nurse notes the client's blood pressure is 190/100 mm Hg. Which medication should the nurse administer first?

    1. nitroglycerin
    2. metoprolol
    3. furosemide
    4. lisinopril

42. The nurse is caring for a client with heart failure and notes edema in the lower extremities. Which nursing intervention would be most appropriate to promote effective tissue perfusion?

    1. Elevating the legs on pillows.
    2. Applying ice packs to the legs.
    3. Providing a low-sodium diet.
    4. Administer diuretics as ordered.

43. The practical nurse is caring for a client with Parkinson's disease. Which assessment finding should the nurse expect related to motor symptoms?

   1. hyperreflexia
   2. resting tremors
   3. hypertonicity
   4. spasticity

44. A client with a head injury is being monitored for signs of increased intracranial pressure. The nurse should be concerned if which finding is observed?

   1. bradycardia
   2. fever
   3. drooling at the mouth
   4. pupillary constriction

45. A client with a urinary tract infection is prescribed trimethoprim-sulfamethoxazole. The nurse should instruct the client to monitor which potential adverse effects of this medication?

   1. hypokalemia
   2. hypernatremia
   3. hematuria
   4. photosensitivity

46. Which finding is consistent with a urinary tract infection?

   1. hypertension
   2. polyuria
   3. hematuria
   4. decreased creatinine levels

47. Which assessment finding is the most important to closely monitor in a client with chronic obstructive pulmonary disease?

   1. respiratory rate
   2. blood pressure
   3. capillary refill
   4. oxygen saturation

48. A client is diagnosed with primary adrenal insufficiency. Which electrolyte imbalance is associated with this condition?

   1. hypernatremia
   2. hypokalemia
   3. hypercalcemia
   4. hypocalcemia

49. A RN is caring for a client with heart failure. Which nursing activity should the registered nurse prioritize to promote fluid balance?

   1. Monitoring daily weights
   2. Administering prescribed diuretics
   3. Assessing with ambulation every two hours
   4. Providing a low-sodium diet

50. The nurse is providing care to multiple clients. Which situation should the nurse address first?

   1. A client who reports severe pain following a surgical procedure.
   2. A client who requires a dressing change
   3. A client who has a newly prescribed medication.
   4. A client who needs assistance with ambulation and transfer.

1. 1-Cytomegalovirus is a serious viral infection of the retina. The retina is the light sensing nerve layer that lines the back of the eye.

2. 2-The assessment findings of detached retina include: flashes of light, floaters, and visual field loss. Patients describe it like a curtain coming across the visual field.

3. 1-As indicated in the clinical name, otitis media is an inflammation of the middle ear.

4. 2-The client with the airway complication should be the priority. Suctioning the client reduces mucous and secretions which can block the airway.

5. 1-Spasms in the larynx is an airway condition that could reduce the client's oxygenation and cause permanent damage.

6. 1-Meniere's disease is a problem with fluid buildup in the ear. A low sodium diet is best to reduce fluid retention.

7. 1-The unlicensed assistive personnel is trained in basic cardiac life support. They are able to give rescue breaths and do chest compressions. The licensed nurse should perform all other tasks.

8. 4-To reduce further exposure to the venom the mother should remove the stinger from the child's skin. This is the priority action. Applying ice and administering pain or allergy reducing medication should follow.

9. 4-Urinary tract infections are a frequent complication in clients with multiple sclerosis because of the effect on bladder function. The elevated temperature suggest that this client may have an infection. The physician should be notified immediately.

10. 4-SIADH is a condition of fluid retention which will cause a sodium deficit leading to hyponatremia.

11. 4-Universal precautions is an approach to infection control to treat all human blood and certain human body fluids as if they were known to be infectious for HIV, HBV, and other bloodborne pathogens.

12. 1 & 5-Parents can place eating utensils in the family dishwasher. Trash should also be taken out on daily basis for clean sanitation. Closed or open mouth kissing does not transmit the HIV virus, uneaten food is safe to be refrigerated and monitoring the child's weight is an appropriate intervention.

13. 1, 3, 4, 5-Renal artery occlusion is blockage of the renal artery may cause symptoms of acute kidney failure. High blood pressure can damage blood vessels in the kidney, reducing their ability to work properly. High blood pressure is the second leading cause of kidney failure after diabetes mellitus. Diabetes can also damage kidneys causing an acute attack to occur.

14. 2-During an allergic reaction a nurse should secure the airway and then immediately contact the physician for new orders that may be needed. All of the other options can be done after the physician is notified.

15. 3-Using furosemide together with vancomycin can increase the risk of kidney and inner ear damage. These effects may be more likely to occur in older adults or those with preexisting kidney problems or dehydration.

16. 1-Steven Johnson syndrome is a serious disorder in which your skin and mucous membranes react severely to a medication or infection. Steven Johnson syndrome often with flu-like symptoms. These are followed by a painful red or purplish rash that spreads and then blisters.

17. 1-Systemic lupus erythematosus is an autoimmune disease in which the body's immune system mistakenly attacks healthy tissue. Symptoms vary but can include fatigue, joint pain, rash, and fever. These can periodically get worse (flare-up) and then improve.

18. 2-Raynaud's disease is characterized by vasospasms of the arteries of the upper and lower extremities.

19. 4-The chancres associated with syphilis are considered a primary symptom that should be expected by the nurse during the assessment findings.

20. 4-Airway obstruction is an indication to surgically create an open airway in the trachea.

21. 2-Cranial nerve IV trochlear is responsible for eye movement. Cranial nerve III Oculomotor and cranial nerve VI abducens is also responsible.

22. 3-Cardiac arrhythmias are a result of malnutrition. This should be an expected complication of cardiac arrhythmias

23. 2,3,4- Patients with COPD are expected to have clubbed fingers, barrel chest, and dyspnea (shortness of breath). Weight loss is more expected than weight gain. Diabetes mellitus type 2 is not expected in clients with COPD.

24. 1-Apnea is an expected sign of newborn hypoglycemia. Other signs of are jitteriness, cyanosis, and tachycardia.

25. 4- Serum levels higher than 12 mg/dl is considered a condition of hyperbilirubinemia.

26. 2-Acyclovir is used to treat active genital herpes.

27. 3- Polycythemia vera is a condition of increased erythrocytes. The most effective treatment is phlebotomy which are blood draws that happens several times a year.

28. 4-Phlebitis is an inflammation of the vein, this is the term that should be documented.

29. 4-Adrenal gland dysfunction can cause pheochromocytoma

30. 1-Administering the bronchodilator is the first action to relieve the child's respiratory distress in an acute asthma exacerbation.

31. 3-Rebound tenderness can be indicative of appendicitis and should be reported immediately for further evaluation.

32. 1-Heart rate is a critical indicator of dehydration in children. Tachycardia is an early sign and can help determine the severity of dehydration.

33. 4-Droplet precautions are required for RSV. RSV is primarily transmitted through respiratory droplets.

34. 1-DKA is characterized by metabolic acidosis due to the accumulation of ketones in the blood.

35. 4-Hyperthyroidism is characterized by an overactive thyroid gland, leading to an increased heart rate, restlessness, and other signs of hyperactivity.

36. 3-Desmopressin is a synthetic form of vasopressin that is used to manage diabetes insipidus by reducing excessive thirst and urination.

37. 4-Diabetes insipidus results in dilute urine with a low specific gravity. A urine specific gravity test can help differentiate between central and nephrogenic causes of the condition.

38. 4-Enoxaparin is an anticoagulant used to prevent and treat blood clots. The primary concern with anticoagulants is the risk of bleeding. The nurse should carefully monitor the client for signs of bleeding such as petechiae, hematomas, and tarry stools.

39. 2-A common adverse effect of ACE inhibitors like lisinopril is a persistent, dry cough. This cough is related to the accumulation of bradykinin and may warrant a medication change if causes negative effects.

40. 2-Warfarin is an anticoagulant commonly prescribed for clients with atrial fibrillation to prevent thrombus formation. Monitoring the PT and INR helps assess their therapeutic effect and the client's anticoagulation status. The INR provides a standardized measure of the PT, allowing for consistent monitoring of anticoagulation.

41. 2-Metoprolol is a beta blocker that helps lower blood pressure and relieve symptoms of hypertension. As the client's blood pressure is elevated and they are experiencing chest pain and shortness of breath, metoprolol should be administered as a priority to reduce blood pressure and improve symptoms.

42. 4-Edema in the lower extremities is often a symptom of heart failure and indicates fluid overload. Administering diuretics as prescribed helps remove excess fluid from the body, promoting effective tissue perfusion.

43. 2-Resting tremors, typically observed in the hands and the fingers are a common motor symptom of Parkinson's disease. The nurse needs to be aware of these characteristics.

44. 1-Bradycardia is a concerning sign in clients with a head injury because it can indicate a rise in intracranial pressure.

45. 4-Trimethoprim-sulfamethoxazole is an antibiotic commonly used to treat UTIs. Photosensitivity is a potential adverse effect, so the client should be educated to use sunscreen and protective clothing when outdoors.

46. 3-Hematuria is a common finding in UTIs. The inflammation and irritation of the urinary tract can cause small blood vessels to leak blood into the urine.

47. 4-Oxygen saturation should be closely monitored in a client with COPD. These clients often have reduced lung function and impaired gas exchange, leading to a decreased oxygen level in the blood.

48. 2-An adrenal insufficiency or Addison's disease can lead to decreased production of aldosterone, causing potassium retention, and consequently hypokalemia.

49. 1-Monitoring daily weights and fluid intake. This activity helps to assess and monitor the fluid balance in clients with heart failure, allowing for early detection of fluid retention and dehydration.

50. 1-A client who reports severe pain following a surgical procedure should be the first as it could be an indication of an urgent or serious complication. The other clients are not the immediate priority.

Take the FINAL Steps to finish Strong!

Get the NCLEX V2

Congratulations on Completing *Quick Facts* for Nursing School®

You're now an official studying member of the ReMar Nurse Family!

Hey ReMar Nurse, so how was it? Have you learned more than you ever thought possible about anatomy, pathophysiology, and pharmacology?

I hope that you've enjoyed your studying experience so far. If this is your first time completing Quick Facts for Nursing School I can tell you that most of my students continue to study with us up until graduation and exit exams!

It was my goal to make this study guide very easy to understand. I believe true education should not drain you. It should bring life, hope, and a better outlook towards reaching your goals.

As I said before, use this as a reference book. Come back to it when you want to study specific topics from the table of contents!

I want to let you know you're on the right track and I'm super proud that you've completed this resource but you're not done yet. I've created an entire system of training with video lectures and Qbanks to take your prep to the next level as you prepare for graduation!

Taking the Next Steps on Your Road to Graduation!

As you can see, *Quick Facts for Nursing School* is an amazing book to help you through your training but WAIT there's more! You may be an audio-visual learner and we have something more for you!

Nursing students also use my video lecture series to get a jump start on nursing school inside of my ReMar Nurse V2 Online Training platform and App!

Check out my website www.ReMarNurse.com to see all my helpful products for nursing students!

I'm also looking for a few special schools that would like the opportunity to train with me for FREE! If your school is interested just give my contact to one of the teachers and have them email me at Support@remarreview.com to find out how we can equip your entire class with the ReMar V2.

Your passion for nursing is a true blessing. It will carry you through the challenges of nursing school and beyond! I'm here for you and can't wait to see your testimony once you pass nursing school!

Professor Regina M. Callion MSN, RN
www.ReMarNurse.com